STEPHEN HARRIS *Designer/Craftsman*

Stephen Harris

DESIGNER/CRAFTSMAN

Hart Massey

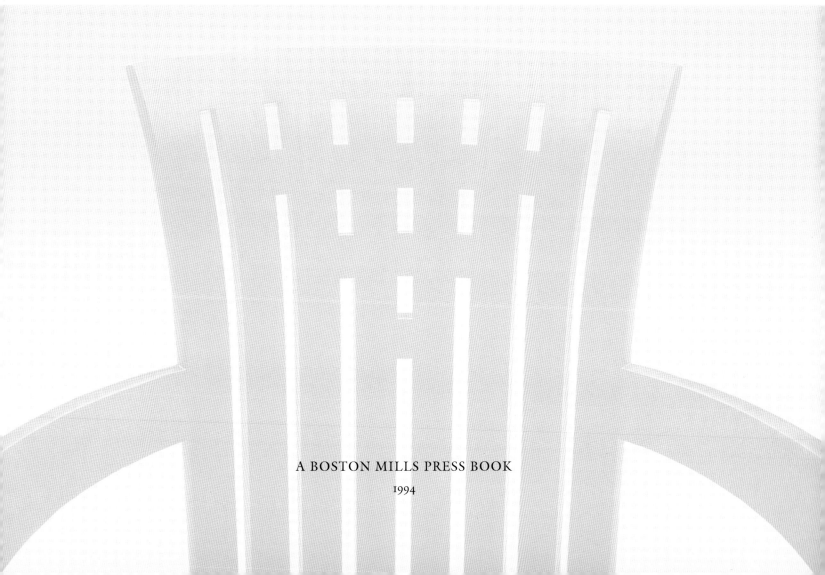

A BOSTON MILLS PRESS BOOK

1994

Canadian Cataloguing in Publication Data

Massey, Hart, 1918–
    Stephen Harris : designer/craftsman

Includes bibliographical references.
ISBN 1-55046-124-9

1. Harris, Stephen, 1939-1991. 2. Furniture –
Canada. 3. Furniture designers – Canada –
Biography. 4. Furniture making – Canada –
Biography.
I. Title

NK2443.H37M37 1994   749.211
C94-931777-2

Privately published by the Stephen Harris
Monograph Committee, 1994

Distributed by The Boston Mills Press/
Stoddart Publishing Co. Limited
34 Lesmill Road
Toronto, Ontario
M3B 2T6
(416) 445-3333

Credits

Editor: Ian Montagnes

Final Editing: Robert Stacey

Inventory of Stephen Harris work: Robert Hill

*Photographs in this book were provided by the following
    individuals:* John Clayson, Kathie Epp, Paul Epp,
    John Flanders, Daphne Harris, Howard Harris,
    Jeff Harris, Stephen Harris, Arnaud Maggs,
    Melodie Massey, Hart Massey, Peter MacCallum,
    Peter Paterson, Ken Tucker, Ted Yarwood.

Book design and typesetting: Adams + Associates
    Design Consultants Inc., Toronto

Type fonts: Galliard and Officina Sans

*Colour separations, film output, printing and
    bindery:* Regent Publishing, Hong Kong

Cloth for cover: Asahi "T" Saifu bookbinding cloth

End-papers: 140 GSM K-Mark Woodfree paper printed
    with overall PMS colour

Bookjacket: 157 GSM Mitsubishi Glossy Art paper
    with overall gloss lamination

Tinted pages: 115 GSM K-Mark Woodfree paper
    printed with overall PMS colours

White pages: 140 GSM Mitsubishi Matt Art paper

This monograph on Stephen Harris owes its existence to the small group of individuals who formed the Stephen Harris Monograph Committee. They were involved in every step along the way, from the original idea to the selection of material for the book, the raising of money to make it possible, and its design and final production. Its members were:

Michael Cruickshank
Paul Epp
Daphne Harris
Hart Massey
Peter Paterson
Molly Thom

The monograph project was supported from the outset by Sheridan College, Oakville, Ontario, with the interest and assistance of Don McKinley, head of the Furniture Program in the School of Crafts and Design at Sheridan since 1967. The role they played was unobtrusive but significant.

As the author, I am particularly grateful to my friend Ian Montagnes whose long experience at the University of Toronto Press well qualified him to perform as editor of my manuscript. He applied his considerable abilities to early drafts, suggesting changes that were of enormous benefit to the final result. My warmest thanks seem hardly enough to repay him for that generous use of his time and skill.

The research and writing phases of the monograph would have been far more difficult, in some cases impossible, without the willing help of many people. Listed elsewhere in the book are all those who were interviewed or wrote to me about Stephen. Their role in this monograph has been vital, and I wish to thank them especially for taking the time to give me so much information about aspects of Stephen's life that otherwise would have been unknown to me. I also owe my gratitude to the members of the Committee, and others who have dutifully reviewed drafts of the text and supplied me with useful comments.

This monograph would never have seen the light of day in book form without the financial support it has received from many sources. We are very grateful for the Ontario Arts Council, the McLean Foundation, the Massey Foundation and the Jackman Foundation both for their interest in the book and for the grants they have provided. We also wish to express our warm thanks to family members, friends, clients and colleagues who have given generously towards this record of Stephen Harris, the man and the craftsman.

Hart Massey
Canton, Ontario, 1994

I first met Stephen Harris in the early 1970s on one of his escapes from Toronto into the wider open spaces around the village of Canton, Ontario, where my wife and I were living. His own mother, father and sister then spent the weekends in their own house, less than a mile from our own, and Stephen occasionally paid them brief visits. He already knew where we lived from our son, a Toronto artist, and one day, in the direct Stephen manner, he simply walked up to our front door, knocked and introduced himself.

It was the first of countless visits over those years, and it was a rare weekend when Stephen wouldn't be at Durham House, sometimes with friends, but mostly by himself. He found it a compatible place, an old house full of beautiful and interesting things, good food, two older but sympathetic companions, both pursuing their own crafts, and fond of Stephen, who soon became a warm friend, almost a second son.

There was always something to do, and Stephen rejoiced in the kind of outdoor labour that was far-removed from the demanding precision of building furniture. He cut down trees, chopped wood, dug the garden and helped erect my large wind-driven sculptures. We cross-country skiied through the woods and skated on our pond in the winter, canoed the Ganaraska and picked fiddleheads in the spring. In the lazier days of summer, we swam and played casual garden badminton, made cider in the fall, and went for long walks at almost any time of year. Stephen was a wonderful and generous friend whose presence will always grace this place. Everything he did here is remembered with affection, even his odd proclivity for breaking more tools than one might reasonably expect from such a meticulous craftsman.

Following his marriage to Daphne Sherrard in 1979, I saw Stephen less often, but he still came to Durham House for short visits, and whenever I could, I went to his workshop in Toronto for a chat about current work. From the day we first met, he remained a good friend, and I am glad that, in a constantly shifting world, I was given the chance to know Stephen as a friend, even for the brief few years that fate allowed.

Some months after Stephen's death, Daphne Harris and a small group of friends decided that his qualities as a man and his achievement as a craftsman deserved the sort of permanent record we hope this book will provide. I accepted Daphne's request to write the text and prepared myself by interviewing people who knew Stephen from different points of view—family, friends, clients and fellow woodworkers. These interviews offered many insights into Stephen Harris, the man and his work, which provided a rich resource when it came to writing the book.

But this is also a book of photographs. They are just as important as the words, if not more so, for much of Stephen's work was never exhibited or even seen by many. It is the photographs, therefore, that will provide the more important and lasting record of his legacy as a contemporary designer and maker of fine wood furniture.

Beginnings

Canton mill-pond.

Canton

A few miles north of the old lake-side town of Port Hope, a rich, patchy quilt of forest and field rolls away in loose folds toward the hazy blue of distant hills. It is a landscape of tilled land, pasture and orchard carved from dense bush many years ago by early settlers. Its hard-won acres stand in defiance of the remaining forest dispersed now in more manageable clumps through much of the township. Here and there, the bald geometry of barn and silo mark the outcroppings of man's tenure of this gentle land. It is rural Ontario at its best, a place blessed with good soil for growing things and the hills, valleys, streams and natural growth that combine to create its special quality.

The settlers came here early in the last century, many of them Methodists from south of the border like Stephen Harris's forebears, looking for a secure life under the English crown. Canton became the focus of a small community mainly because of the land, and the power that lay waiting in the Ganaraska River whose two branches joined there. Trees were in abundance then, even those tall and straight enough for Royal Navy masts, and lumber was badly needed for building almost everything.

The village was never, even in its heyday, the compact, companionable huddle of dwellings that the word conjures in the mind. It was always spread thinly on the ground and remains so today, reaching into the country nearby to claim its present residents. Many of the old village buildings are now gone, but Canton still carries on with an identity preserved by its small, scattered but loyal population—a survival that is due more, perhaps, to the inhabitants' attitude of mind than to anything more tangible.

Stephen's ancestor, Myndert Harris, arrived with his family in 1793 at what was then Smith's Creek, the antecedent of the present-day Port Hope. Eighteen years later, his son, also Myndert, bought the first hundred acres of the farm where Stephen's family now lives. Stephen knew Canton and Hope Township well. As a boy, he spent many summer days there, and throughout his life, he returned time and again to refresh himself in its rich, rolling countryside.

. . .

24 August 1991　　The Harris house lies on a little-used sideroad near the sturdy brick United Church and its neighbour, the Community Hall, at one time Canton's first Methodist Church. Across the road from them is the remarkable Canton cemetery, a small but rare and tranquil precinct where old family gravestones recall the village's long history.

The cemetery sits on the edge of the Ganaraska valley, the ground falling away to the river on the south and west. To the east lies an orchard, its trees in late August heavy with ripening apples. Ancient sugar maples define the two long sides of the narrow graveyard, and straight down the centre marches a formal avenue of pyramidal cedars planted close together in two uncompromising rows—a kind of formal graveyard landscaping seen more often in Europe than rural Ontario. Like the maples, the cedars have been there a long time and now extend their slender dark green shafts twenty feet or more above the grass. This narrow central avenue is the cemetery's dominant feature. More than anything, it creates the special quality of the place, giving it a scale, a presence, even a monumentality it would otherwise lack. It is, in large part, responsible for the atmosphere of dignity and peace visitors sense when they walk through the cemetery gates.

In a moving tribute to the man, it was to this church and this cemetery that more than two hundred people came one day in late summer to say their farewells to Stephen Harris who had died on 20 August 1991 at fifty-two, following a bicycle accident in Toronto. They came because of Stephen the craftsman, the designer and maker of furniture, and because of Stephen the man, whose rare qualities they had learned to cherish. Most had driven many miles to Canton, feeling compelled to be there because of what knowing Stephen had meant to every one of them.

After a short service in the packed church, we slowly walked across the road and down the long avenue of cedars to stand in silent groups near the grave. It was a bright, still afternoon. The canopy of maples high above cast dark pools of shade to relieve the dazzling green of the sunlit grass. There was no wind. Nothing stirred, not even the leaves. The sentinel cedars stood motionless in the background. A bird flew silently overhead but was soon gone. The few words spoken at the grave were the only sounds, the sole intruders in those minutes of absolute stillness. When at last it was over, the little groups

19

of standing figures stayed motionless for a while longer, then quietly, very slowly and almost reluctantly began to leave the cemetery in twos and threes. It seemed to take a long time before we had all strolled down the road to gather again on the lawn of the Harris house.

. . .

"You Aren't the Boss of Me!"

Stephen arrived in the Harris family on 8 June 1939, the last and youngest of the two boys and two girls comprising the younger generation. His father, Howard Harris, was to spend his entire working life, from sixteen-year-old junior clerk to chairman of the board, in the same Toronto dental-supply company. Stephen's mother, Edith, was a gentle, well-mannered woman with an interest in music who kept the routines of life ticking over smoothly in the house the family occupied for forty-three years in the affluent Toronto enclave of Forest Hill Village.

It was there, under the firm authoritarian leadership of Howard, that they lived their lives by a strict code of behaviour reflecting the conventions of the conformist, United Church constituency to which they belonged. It was an orderly, unadventurous existence revolving around the obligations of business, school and church, but a restrictive one, especially for the children. It was certainly not a household in which unusual plants would be encouraged to bloom. Nor was it likely to accept much disruption from its most junior member.

It may have taken Stephen a few years to size the situation up, but once well beyond the diaper stage, he would have sensed the general drift of life at 422 Russell Hill Road and might, understandably, have concluded that he was in the wrong place. The strong-willed little rebel didn't like the rigidly enforced rules or the discipline that came with them. He undoubtedly also entertained some reservations about his inflexible father, whose ideas so often conflicted with his own.

As sons often do, the growing Stephen increasingly extracted boyish thrills from the constant needling of his father, pushing matters as far as they could go, often right to the point of a parental outburst. But in Stephen these mini-jousts had a significance beyond the game itself. They were the early flexings of that will whose strength would be a dominant feature of the later man, as would a taste for the tricky ground right at the limits of prudence.

Stephen at sixteen, from a Harris family photograph, c. 1955.

It was inevitable that stern father and combative young son should meet head-on. Even at a very tender age, Stephen's diminutive figure once stood boldly in front of his towering father and answered a reprimand with the decisive: "You aren't the boss of me!" It was a gutsy, even rash gesture of defiance. Probably not much was achieved by it at the time, but, for Stephen, it was an important manifesto, one destined to be a foretaste of future father/son relations. It also symbolized what would become his abiding attitude towards authority, and a fierce determination to govern his own affairs. Both were to accompany him throughout life.

. . .

Growing Up   Stephen was a bright boy but showed little interest in the classroom and did not shine there. He was, however, popular, had lots of friends and shared their enthusiasms. He played the usual seasonal games but, as he became older, increasingly favoured individual sports over the team ones, and, later, in his teens became absorbed in figure skating for about two years. It was not then (or perhaps even now) a common sport for a boy, and his interest in it might have been thought unusual by his peers. But Stephen was indifferent to what others thought, and was understandably attracted to the grace and flowing movement of ice-dancing with a girl partner.

There seem to have been few hobbies or special interests in Stephen's boyhood years. The country around Canton was, however, another matter. Howard's family spent many weekends and the long summer holidays in a cottage on the property. These were rewarding days for a young boy. A fresh and different sort of life beckoned in country wide-open for exploration, rich in woods, running water, birds, animals and, most important of all, an abundance of surprises and secret places. It was during those years that Stephen first came to know the forests, meadows and streams near Canton and unconsciously built the foundation of a love for them that nourished him throughout his life.

By the time Stephen was fourteen, poor results at school convinced his father that a move to Upper Canada College might better his chances of passing the approaching provincial exams. The three-and-a-half years Stephen spent in the large private school were not a success. He found himself at odds with its old-fashioned ways and some of the values it fostered. He particularly resented the all-pervasive presence of authority, the prefect system, the regimentation of sport, the forced discipline of the school Battalion, and recoiled from the eccentric teaching methods adopted by some masters.

Fortunately for Stephen, Upper Canada College at least gave him friends and, through them, some measure of release from the difficulties he faced there, and in the increasingly confining atmosphere at home. They were a small group, held together by common interests and an urge to extract all they could from life. Most came from affluent families, more liberal with their allowances than the Harrises seemed to be. His friends considered him the poor one of the group, but in spite of that it was Stephen who first bought

Stephen at seventeen in
the Battalion uniform of
Upper Canada College,
Toronto, Ontario.

a motorcycle, "a little English putt-putt." The next one to have a motorbike
was Ian Griffin. Being too young for a licence, he used to sneak downstairs
at 2.00 in the morning, get on his bike, roll it silently out of the garage and
down the street before starting it to zoom off into the Toronto night with
Stephen. It wasn't long before they all had motorbikes. Their enthusiasm for
these machines and the freedom they offered formed an important bond.

Except for the friends made there, Stephen was anxious to put the school
behind him. At last, in December 1958, his departure was forced by the
school, when he was asked to leave half-way through his grade-thirteen year.
The school told his father that Stephen was disruptive in class, although one
of his friends disputed that claim and thought of him more as an occasional
prankster. Whatever the reason, he left UCC, and successfully completed his
grade thirteen at a cram school in June of the following year.

During the years at UCC, Stephen made the passage from boy to early manhood. In the process, he sharpened and reinforced the character traits that were to become pronounced in later life. He was already a confirmed nonconformist and sometime rebel, having started early on the path of resisting authority wherever it impinged on him. He was even then truly independent in thought and action, not even always sharing the same interests as his friends, and determined more than ever to do things his own way. He already had a keen appetite for adventure, and a yearning for horizons far broader than the limitations of family and home town. An easy-going nature and gentleness of manner, combined with a sense of humour and a generous spirit, made Stephen popular with others. He made friends easily and was never short of them. Even in his clothes he showed the same personal restraint and attention to detail that later became typical of him. As a boy at UCC, Stephen was always perfectly groomed, regularly riding his motorbike in spotless grey flannels, tweed jacket, shirt, tie and highly polished shoes.

. . .

24

Journeys

During the summer months, Stephen often went off with friends on expeditions. They varied from gentle cruises on Ontario waterways to a long-range and somewhat hazardous adventure thousands of miles to the south. But in the summer of 1958 it was something quite different and uniquely Canadian.

That year, Stephen and his friend Ian Griffin sailed as cabin boys on a government icebreaker during its long summer voyage into the high Arctic. It was a special kind of adventure, through an unfamiliar and exciting world, taking them as far north as Eureka on Ellesmere Island, only 300 miles from the North Pole. Whenever they could, they explored the land on long walks toward the distant horizon, the Arctic air so clean and clear that everything looked closer than it really was. They were fascinated by an experience then relatively unknown to most Canadians and, on their return, talked enthusiastically about it to others. Disappointingly, they found few receptive listeners.

As so often happened with his friends, it was Stephen who first suggested the trip to Mexico. He was always hungry for the new, the adventurous, the exciting, and a trip to Mexico on motorbikes seemed to offer all of these. If serious risk was thrown in as well, that, too, was fine with Stephen.

Eventually, it was also Stephen who decided that the classic English "Matchless" was THE BIKE for the trip. He bought a brand-new 650cc twin which Ian thought a magnificent machine, and acquired a second-hand 600cc "Matchless" for himself. They had been warned about Mexico by a friend living there. He knew it could be a dangerous place, with poverty so bad that travellers in the mountains could be killed just for the chrome on their bikes, and suggested they at least be armed. Taking this advice, Ian concealed his father's Smith and Wesson .38 carefully but almost inextricably under the seat of his bike. The fact that he didn't know how to use it seemed at the time of little importance. After careful planning, they at last set off in the summer of 1959 for three months on the road, each with $150 in cash and a credit card for gas. They camped through the United States, but in Mexico were more cautious, using whatever shelter they could find.

As they went further south, sun-spangled Mexico erupted around them with all its scenic excitements, warm-hearted people, rare delights, surprises and dangers. They made friends, met women, had a roadside encounter with vultures, bumped over a giant snake lying like a fire-hose across the road, narrowly missed dropping into the frequent cave-ins on minor roads, had a near-fatal skid on the lip of a deep ravine, were robbed in Acapulco, and took part in a bizarre race across the mountains with two sporty types in fast cars.

Near the U.S. border on the way home, Stephen's English bike broke down and they sought help from the Mexican police to get it to Texas for repairs. Surprisingly helpful, a policeman stopped a truck, told the driver to put the bike inside and take it to San Antonio. The truck's load of Coca-Cola bottles was pushed aside, and with Stephen looking on anxiously, his immaculate bike was roughly shoved in. The truck then took off and drove night and day to San Antonio. With Stephen riding pillion, Ian followed the truck closely, keeping it constantly in sight for fear of losing Stephen's bike forever.

After thirty-six hours' steady driving, they arrived in San Antonio at three in the morning, completely bushed. Leaving Stephen's bike near the repair shop, they pitched their tent on a green lawn on the outskirts of town. Once in the deepest of sleeps, the tent was violently ripped open. Blinking sleepily from their mummy bags, they faced a flashlight, a pointed gun and fears that the very worst was about to happen. A voice then bellowed: "What the hell are you guys doing?" With relief they found the voice belonged to a policeman, a tough but understanding cop who allowed them to stay the night if they left early the next day.

The repairs, once done and paid for, left the two with only seven dollars in cash. They had the credit cards for gas but they were still two thousand miles from Toronto, and seven dollars wouldn't buy much food. The prospect was not good but they found a place where, amazingly, one dollar could buy seven hamburgers. So they spun out the forty-nine hamburgers by eating   half a one for each meal and made it safely home at last. It had been a major effort and one of the turning points in both their lives, giving them the confi-dence to do things from then on that weren't just run-of-the-mill. It was the start of a breaking away. Stephen, the adventurous one, more than any of his friends was responsible for getting them to do the seemingly crazy things that, with-out his prompting, they would never have dreamt of.

The third journey was quite unlike the others, being short, tranquil and closer to home, but belongs here because of the amusing light it casts on Stephen. Summer boat or canoe trips had become an annual event for Stephen and his friends. In 1961 four of them rented two sixteen-foot boats at Kingston, went down the St. Lawrence to Montreal, then up the Ottawa River, and returned to Kingston via the Rideau waterway. Somewhere on the Rideau, they camped for the night outside a dozy little town. On the main street, every house had its front porch with people rocking back and forth, enjoying the quiet evening at day's end.

Earlier, his friends had been casually talking about Stephen's shortage of cash. Deciding to put up ten dollars each, they challenged him to go down the main street with no clothes on. Because of all the people watching from porches, they assumed that he might not accept the dare at all, or, if he did, would certainly run as fast as he could. But he immediately accepted, walked to the end of the main street, went behind a tree and re-appeared, ready for the challenge.

Stephen started off, not running but boldly, even happily sauntering down the main street with his clothes held in a bundle high above his head and unmistakably stark naked. He seemed quite relaxed as he strolled along, singing to himself and occasionally talking to the surprised citizens on their porches to right and left. No one knew how to react or what to do and nothing happened until he had almost reached the end of the street. Then some boys discovered what was going on and took off after him. He at last began to run and hid in some bushes, where neither the boys nor his friends could find him. Shortly after, he showed up at the boats and collected his thirty dollars.

. . .

Passport used by Stephen
in his early twenties before
the first trip to England,
1960.

Breaking Away

Stephen Harris was twenty when he passed his grade thirteen exams in 1959. But what he wanted to do with his life was still not clear. He would try a lot of things before making that decision, but of one thing he was absolutely sure: whatever it was, he'd be doing it on his own.

In November 1959 Stephen joined the Royal Canadian Air Force as a flight cadet. He had simply done it, without even telling his parents. Flying would have had a strong appeal for Stephen. The rebel's dream of flying free above the clouds was, however, rapidly grounded by the hard work and discipline of an Air Force Elementary Flying Training Unit where authority, Stephen's particular *bête noire* was all-pervasive. He was not to be a success either in the air or in the classroom, and his final assessment was littered with unfavourable comments. The RCAF was clearly not keen about Stephen and, after four-and-a-half months, he was released in April 1960, no doubt lacking equal enthusiasm for the air force.

28

In the summer of 1960 Stephen conceived the idea that he and Mike Cruickshank should go to England. Such a thought had never crossed his friend's mind but Stephen was persuasive. So they packed up, got on a boat and arrived in Liverpool. Mike was surprised at how easily he had been convinced, but realized they had to break out of their narrow group of friends in Toronto, and knows now that it was one of the best things they ever did.

They had some money but, as always, not enough, and no definite plans. They spent two days in a hostel and then settled into a boarding house in Notting Hill Gate. The strange new world of London was a revelation to them both and, for a while, they simply wandered around, eyes wide-open with wonder, soaking it all up. When their money ran out at the end of the year, they both got jobs as rod-men with a surveying company. For the next few months they worked during the week on surveys all around the south of England and were brought back to London for the week-end. They couldn't have wished for a better arrangement.

This lasted until the summer, each working with a particular surveyor. Most were ex-British Army types, but Stephen was with a surveyor who was quieter and more sensitive than the others. Occasionally the two crews met for lunch, but one day Stephen's crew didn't join the other as planned. It turned out that his boss had just committed suicide. It was shattering news for Stephen, who was much affected by the sudden loss of someone who, in only two months, had become a friend.

In London, they stayed in bed-sitting rooms, three different ones on a descending scale of attractiveness as the money ran low. They spent most of their time going to the theatre, to concerts, to films and art galleries—the fruits of a sophisticated society they hadn't encountered in that way before. It amounted to a concentrated dose of cultural nourishment that their earlier life in Toronto had denied them. Although Stephen knew more about art, music and film than his friend, neither had been exposed to much, and what extra money they had went to broaden these horizons. London was an illuminating new experience, an awakening that had an important influence on them both.

After England and the cosmopolitan riches of London, the University of New Brunswick in Fredericton must have seemed to Stephen like pretty weak tea. Higher learning of a kind, however, was his next attempt at pathfinding, so Stephen and his friend Chuck Coutts started at UNB in the fall of 1961. Stephen, being then several years older than his fellow undergraduates, didn't take easily to the juvenile fun-and-games of freshman life, and rejected many of the university's customs and conventions. He complained about them, didn't agree with them and simply refused to take part.

1. From Stephen Harris's submission on his nomination by the Ontario Crafts Council for the 1989 Saidye Bronfman Award.

As Stephen himself said in a biographical note, "One year at the University of New Brunswick discouraged an interest in scholarship while encouraging an interest in theatre on a full time basis."[1] Stephen got his year, left UNB and turned his attention to what seemed a far more promising activity. He spent the following year in Toronto, where he built sets and worked with set-designers for the Straw Hat Players, a repertory company playing during the summer at Port Carling on Lake Rosseau, in the Muskoka cottage country north of Toronto.

Stephen was beginning at last to discover something he really liked to do. He enjoyed working with wood, the creative, lively atmosphere of the theatre, and the people he met there. It was only a short step for him to think of bringing these interests together in the broader world of the English stage.

Stephen returned to England alone in 1963, just as the cultural revolution of the Sixties was bursting forth. For someone raised with his background, it was a stimulating climate to be in. The signals of radical change were every-where—long hair, jeans, the Beatles, pot and hash, Carnaby Street, a free wheeling life-style, new popular music and all the things that accompanied these symbols of youth's reaction to conservative parental values. It was a blast of fresh air that would, in time, change society.

Stephen first found work as a freelance set-designer and property maker with regional theatre companies, but eventually moved to London, where he found similar employment in the West End. There, he worked for the National Theatre on the south bank of the Thames, the Royal Opera House, Covent Garden, and the Royal Court Theatre in Sloane Square. For the Royal Court, he helped paint the sets designed by David Hockney for the Alfred Jarry play *Ubu Roi*. He also constructed props, including a large, sturdy table, for a strangely cast production of *Macbeth*, with Alec Guinness in the lead and Simone Signoret, the film actress, playing opposite him. The Lady Macbeth of this production had no previous stage experience, and must surely have surprised her audience with lines spoken in a charming French accent. The critics were not kind.

Since the Royal Court had no workshops of its own, Stephen used shops near Blackfriar's Bridge, south of the Thames, entailing frequent trips back and forth across the city in an old jeep-like vehicle oddly powered by an ever-thirsty Rolls-Royce engine. Unfortunately, it is only little snippets like this that survive from that time, and not much else is known about Stephen's life during those five years. Nevertheless, it was clearly a formative period for him. The theatre taught him much about working a variety of materials but, more importantly, he gained an awareness of the high level of craftsmanship achieved by the men with whom he shared the work.

On Stephen's return to Canada in 1968, he got a job as property maker with the Drama Department of the University of Alberta in Edmonton. Both in Edmonton and, later, in Toronto, Stephen met furniture-makers who sparked his interest in that craft. It immediately appealed to him because it brought

together his love of working with wood, a chance to expand the skills he had
started to learn in England, and showed the way to the achievement of the
worthwhile, long-term goal he had been seeking for some time. The thought
of a career designing and making furniture suddenly became an exciting
prospect. After many years of searching, he had found his way at last.

Work

Starting

In 1969 Stephen Harris rented a small space on John Street
in Toronto and began his life as a maker of furniture. But it was a very tentative start, involving the construction of kitchen cabinets and kindred utilitari-
an pieces to keep the workshop solvent. He disliked the work, however, and
soon took the first steps towards his eventual goal of making fine furniture
for private clients. These early pieces took much of their character from the
flat pieces of wood with which they were made—right-angular constructions,
carefully made but lacking any personal flavour. Stephen was held back in
what he could do by his tools, his limited woodworking knowledge, and a
lack of exposure to the broader horizons of his craft.

36

This began to change as increasing familiarity with the burgeoning arts and crafts community in Toronto brought Stephen in touch with artists and craftsmen, among them David Long, a prominent potter, with whom Stephen briefly shared a house. And Fred Ball, a Sheridan College student then working in Stephen's shop, opened his eyes to Wendell Castle, a major figure among American furniture-makers. Paul Epp also played an important role, when working part-time for Stephen, by exposing him to a variety of woodworking tools and techniques which until then were unfamiliar to him.

Also in 1969, Stephen had met Stephen Hogbin, an industrial designer, who had come from England a year before to teach at Sheridan College under Don McKinley. The two Stephens saw each other socially, and talked at length about their mutual interests. They became friends and eventually established a professional association when, in October 1970, they started sharing a workshop at 11 Nelson Street. It was in those early days that Hogbin was a strong influence on Harris.

Stephen Hogbin had a well-trained mind, manipulated design ideas with ease, and had an ability to illustrate them with a pencil. His influence on Stephen Harris was, however, more intellectual than technical. He introduced a needed element of unorthodoxy into Stephen's thinking and provided a stimulating presence in the workshop, whose lathe he used to turn the innovative shapes that absorbed him at the time. After about two years, the two Stephens moved to a larger space at 86 Nelson Street, where they were joined by Bill Hayes and Paul Epp, the latter being a recent graduate of the Furniture Program at Sheridan.

Stephen Hogbin:

Paul's quiet, thoughtful approach would be a tremendous asset to the group. The long conversations I had with Stephen [Harris] shifted to a stronger dialogue between Stephen and Paul. It was a very successful group, and cemented the idea of the cooperative work space, in this case with the leadership coming from Stephen Harris.

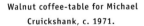

Walnut coffee-table for Michael Cruickshank, c. 1971.

**Cocobolo tray,
1973.**

Paul Epp had earlier worked in spare moments for Stephen, but was now a full partner in the workshop, carrying out his own commissions. He had the benefit of three years formal training, and in some respects knew more about the craft of woodworking than Stephen, who had never received formal instruction and had little furniture-making experience.

P a u l   E p p :

Stephen's range of expertise was restricted but he was very shrewd at figuring things out. After looking at something he usually understood pretty well how it was made. I think that allowed him to teach himself. I learned a lot from him and I like to think he learned a bit from me as well. He probably benefited from my direct exposure to woodworking during three years at Sheridan but it was reciprocal, more me learning from him than the other way round.

38

**Square white oak coffee-
table, 1973.**

Ash reception desk for Robert Burns and Heather Cooper, 1973.

At the beginning, Stephen didn't really see himself as a furniture
maker so much as a handy person who could make things. He was
already a competent maker, but less so in some areas than others.
He gave credit to one or more of the senior British craftsmen he had
worked with in the London theatre who understood about making
things in the traditional sense and making them right. Stephen said
he learned a great deal from them, and not just about props and sets.
Because of his interest, they nurtured him in a broader way.

White elm conference
table for Robert Burns and
Heather Cooper, 1973.

I was alongside Stephen, and able to see him evolve as a furniture
designer. He was reluctant at first to change his self-image, but gradually gathered confidence that he could do it. Holding him back at
first was his inability to draw. He didn't entirely trust his intuition so
he felt he needed to draw to help him understand. He set out to learn
how to draw and finished being able to draw very well. It was a tentative start, building on small successes. He would try things, take a
small chance, then another one, and another and so on. He emerged
quite gradually as a designer and maker.

Stephen was completely consistent in one thing. Whatever he did, he always did it his way, whether in the designing or the making. He was very stubborn about whatever he did. It was the Stephen Harris way, and sometimes he paid dearly for that stubbornness. In the evolution of his design he had to solve all the problems himself. He had to work through it completely on his own. It was as if he almost refused to accept help, although at times he had to ask for it because he got himself into corners he couldn't get out of.

Stephen believed there was an absolute right way to do things. He wanted to achieve absolute truth or rightness. I remember one conversation when he asked me how to resolve a technical detail. I said, "There are a number of ways you can do it." I told him he could do this or that or something else. But he said: "I don't want to know that, I want to know the right way to do it." I replied, "Stephen, there is no one right way, there are many ways. The right way is what you decide is right." But that didn't satisfy him. "No," he said, "that is not true. There is an absolute right that I aspire to and it's not personal. It's like it exists beyond me, something bigger than me." I never did really know what he meant by that, but it was certainly a critical component of Stephen's attitude to his craft that reinforced his stubbornness and determination to do it right.

. . .

Letter from Virginia

Bill Hayes, an American from Virginia, came to Toronto in 1968, only a few weeks before he was to be drafted for service in Viet Nam. Preferring anonymity over a job in the corporate world, for which he was well qualified, he used his woodworking skills to earn a living, first as a plant carpenter and later a freelance woodworker, doing what jobs he could find through friends. He stayed in Toronto for ten years.

Bill Hayes:

I met Stephen at a party in 1971. He and I talked for an hour that first night and through him I began to realize that woodworking could be a worthy, lifelong pursuit. I had a run-down house in Cabbagetown with a simple basement workshop and no machinery. Stephen invited me to drop by his shop, the first of his Nelson Street shops, then shared with Hogbin, a woodturner. Within a week I was there again.

1. In woodworking, jigs are normally made of wood cut to the desired shape and used as guides for power- or hand-tools in the shaping of the final wooden members to ensure accuracy and, in some cases, uniformity. In complex assemblies, they are often used with clamps to hold pieces in the right relationship to each other, and to apply equal pressure on the glued joints.

This was my first introduction to a woodworking shop and though it seemed impressive at the time, it contained only a borrowed 8" table saw, a Beaver drill-press, a 14" band-saw and a small lathe. What was most noticeable were all the jigs[1] Stephen had devised to expand the capabilities of each machine. Also the reverence he bestowed on each tool. He had recently built a vertical cabinet to house his hand tools, arranged and polished as precisely as the cabinet was made.

Stephen was so very gracious and helpful that first day. He helped me cut some plywood so I could assemble it in my basement. He showed me what he was working on, what Hogbin was doing, and I remember thinking how interesting and exciting it was. My visits became more frequent after that, and Stephen became my mentor as well as my friend.

As a mentor, Stephen encouraged me to build a classical guitar, lent me a book about it and let me make parts for it in his shop. I don't think he ever knew how much he taught me because he didn't focus on how much he knew, but more on what he didn't know. I was just one of many who benefited from knowing him.

I think it was in 1972 or '73 that Stephen approached me about sharing a new workshop at 86 Nelson Street. Paul Epp was also coming in, so, with Hogbin, that made four of us. I knew I was being included to help with the rent because as a craftsman I didn't belong on the same block with those guys. All the same, I was flattered to be asked, readily accepted, and felt as if I had just been promoted to a corner office with a window and a view.

And what a view I had. It was my good fortune to watch and work with three of Canada's most prominent emerging woodworkers. Our shop quickly became a resource and learning centre where new ideas were disseminated and new directions forged. One could not help but assimilate the talents of the others. Fine woodworking was becoming more appreciated and Stephen was one of the bolder forces leading the way.

44

During the Seventies, a typical day for Stephen would unfold with breakfast at Barney's on Queen Street, followed by his arrival in the shop around 9:15, the *Globe and Mail* under his arm. Stephen was a slow starter, doing his best work in the afternoon or early evening. If he was ready to glue something at 11 AM, it seemed like he dawdled the time away, postponing the final act to the end of the day. He was nearly always the last to leave. When I arrived first the next morning, I examined his progress and would be amazed at the elaborate clamping jigs he had put in place the night before to apply pressure where it was needed. When I questioned him later he would respond with a casual "It's not easy, mate!" Then he would explain all the problems

he had to overcome, chastising himself for being such a klutz not to see the problems earlier.

Stephen made much use of jigs. He spent considerable time devising and perfecting them. Jigs were his way through a piece—a step-by-step process that guided him in uncharted waters and helped him avoid troubles ahead. With so much at stake, each step entailed careful reckoning, even an act of faith before proceeding. If one word could define Stephen, I would offer "courageous," for he constantly risked failure in his work. With Stephen, nothing easy was ever worth doing.

. . .

The Blank Piece of Paper

Once Stephen had overcome his doubts about being a designer as well as a maker of furniture, he soon began producing pieces worthy of inclusion in exhibitions. He showed work each year between 1971 and 1976. A cherry table, one of the first pieces to show his emergence as a designer/craftsman in his own right, was in an exhibition with work by Paul Epp at the Canadian Guild of Crafts (Ontario) in 1974; it was the first furniture show at a craft gallery in Toronto, perhaps even in Canada. The table won a Design Canada Award of Merit. Stephen's work was starting to be noticed, and the first clients for his special kind of furniture were appearing with serious commissions. Stephen was at last embarked on the path he would follow throughout the rest of his life. But before any commission could be confirmed or the making begin, some important preliminary moves had to be played out.

Stephen Harris:

The first move in a possible commission is only someone saying: "I like what you do. Can we do this?" It may or may not work out. We have a great deal to agree on before the commission is definite. I guess the most boring thing is trying to determine whether we understand each other, whether they understand my limitations, what I can or cannot do for them, what they will accept in terms of cost and style. From talking with them, and seeing where they live, I can get a fair idea of whether we can work together and whether something I did would look horrible or comfortable there. I try not to get into matters of taste because they know the kind of work I do. I can only stretch a tiny bit to accommodate someone else's taste.

You have to be able to communicate with a client. We have to like each other a little because I need their help through the design process. An object has to satisfy a functional need, and blend in one way or another with things the client already has. So, to some extent, I have to play the role of decorator, but am not comfortable in that role.

Certainly it's more rewarding when the client has some knowledge of furniture, of materials, how things are made, and why they are made, because ninety percent of my time is in the making. For eight hours a day and as many days as it takes, I am concerned with what happens between the wood, my two hands and a machine. It is nice if a client is interested enough to come and look at the piece as it develops, and has some understanding of why so much time is going into it.

There is some trepidation when I am staring at a blank piece of paper, and wondering where to start. But once I get going, I know that, sooner or later, either from the client's prompting or just from previous experience, I'll get a thread of something that will eventually work into a design. I hope that it will happen the first time, but it seldom does.

I know I am not going to perform any magic at a drawing board. I also know that if an object can come together on a piece of paper it requires a great deal of confidence, and I don't feel confident much of the time. For one finished drawing there are probably twenty or more that must be thrown away and hundreds of little sketches of ideas for details and searches for something that will work.

Square cherry table with cylindrical
legs for B. and H. Thomas, 1974.
One of Stephen's earliest
innovative pieces.

48

It is paramount that I am happy with the solution. I could not pro-
ceed if I wasn't; there is too much hard work ahead. If, in my terms,
I'm not certain that it is a good piece of design, I simply couldn't do
it. For me, to solve a problem is to please myself first, and then to
please the client.

In design, I initially try to ignore the details of joinery and do sketches
as if the piece were to be made in clay or plastic and totally malleable.
I think the rigidity of wood can get in the way, and inhibit the freedom
of your thinking. Once I have the outline of a piece, I ask myself how
can I make it, because you can get into very bad problems. In fact, you
may have drawn something that is so difficult to make that it may cost

**Detail of cherry table showing
the corner detail.**

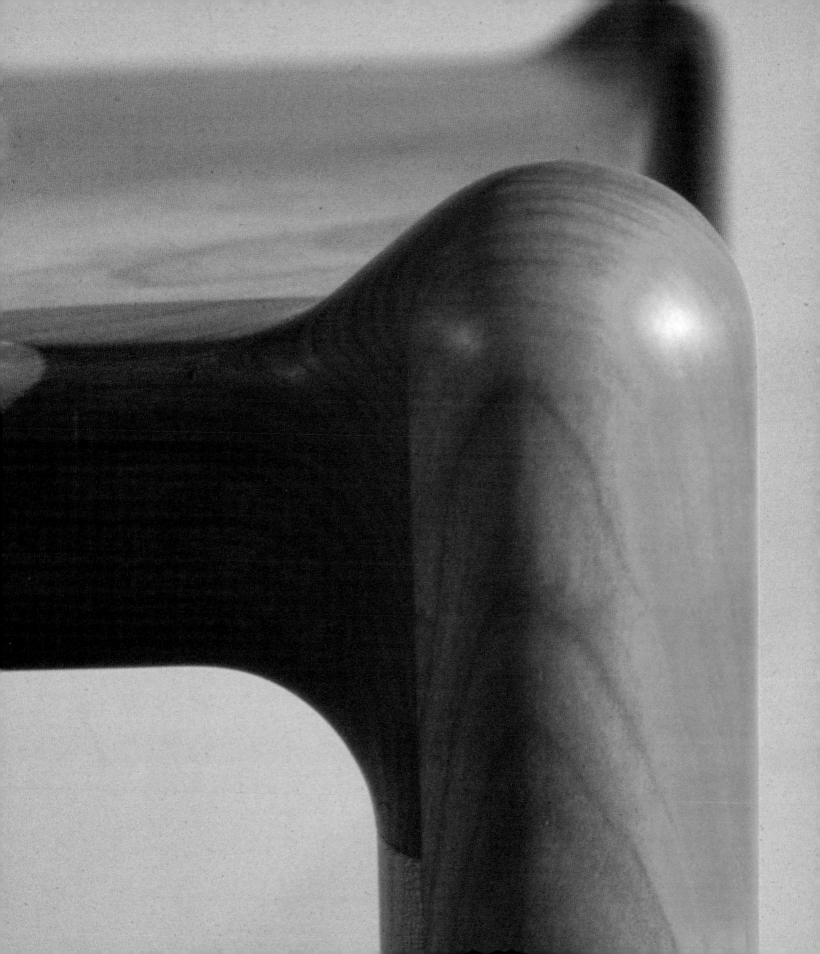

twice what you estimate or, even worse, you may not be able to solve the problems in any reasonable fashion. I have sometimes even come right to the brink of committing myself to a project, and find there is no way out but putting ten times the number of hours into it that I wanted or calculated. So I try to foresee the possible difficulties in the design stage.

When the drawing is finished and approved by the client, it is like reaching a kind of plateau. I can then launch myself into the next and most important stage, which is making the piece. It is very satisfying to get there because the design is almost always a very difficult part for me. But once I start in the workshop, the really serious work begins. I have the design outline, and I am pretty sure I can make the piece, but there is a strong possibility that I have ignored a few difficulties that are going to cost me later.[1]

1. From an interview by Alastair Brown in Stephen's Toronto Workshop.

50

When Stephen began as a furniture-maker, his approach to design was uncertain and tentative. He knew, in vague terms, the general direction he favoured, but found specific designs to achieve it harder to realize. The Art Nouveau furniture that he saw in books and during travel in Europe in 1976 on a Canada Council grant had the sculptural, organic quality that appealed to him, but much of it seemed overdone, too literal in its embellishments, and often demanded a wood-carver's skills. He found Art Nouveau too blatant in its use of natural forms, and in his own work wanted them to be suggested rather than overt. It was never a strong influence on his furniture, and although occasional hints of it occurred in some pieces, he soon left it behind. Stephen was, however, concerned about a possible misunderstanding of his work, and wrote in the mid-Seventies: "There is a danger of implying another time in my work [i.e., the Art Nouveau era] without having the intent of that work. This can probably be avoided with care and building on what I have learned, slowly." And, through slow evolution, he did develop a style that was his own. Based to some extent on tradition and without forcing or striving for originality, that style came about almost naturally. He just worked away at it by himself, slowly and steadily.

Probably the earliest piece that broke into new territory was a bed he made for a friend. It had cylindrical legs, set out from the frame, with which they made a graceful transition. The cherry table that won the 1974 Design Canada Award also used this design idea. Shortly after completing these pieces, Stephen started receiving major commissions, particularly from Robert Burns, a graphic designer, and his wife, Heather Cooper, a graphic designer and illustrator; both were strong Stephen supporters in the 1970s, helping him in several ways. Through these commissions, he soon became more adventurous in design and slowly evolved his personal style. Furniture he made in the mid-Seventies for the Perlitz and Gorman families and some trays and mirrors he entered in the 1974 Design Canada exhibition also revealed for the first time a more organic approach to form and the use of thoughtful, sensuous, even sensual details that marked much of his subsequent work.

With increasing confidence, Stephen left hard geometry behind, denying and disguising the inherently geometric evidence of machine-tool operations. His furniture became a fluid expression of carefully fitted components unobtrusively joined together to form a single, sensual whole. The legs of tables and chairs continually changed to become lighter and more organic in form. And to relieve the flatness of elements that must be flat, Stephen painstakingly devised a process of inlaying and joining parts along the graceful curves he liked to incorporate in his work. As his sureness in design grew he began to focus as well on the smaller details—transitions and junctions, incising and inlaying.

Stephen has left very few of his own words to help explain what he aimed to achieve in his furniture. To a very great extent, the pieces themselves must speak for him. He did, however, leave behind a few thoughts about his work in brief interviews for various publications.

S t e p h e n   H a r r i s :

2. Stephen Harris, quoted in Hart Massey and John Flanders, *The Craftsman's Way* (Toronto: University of Toronto Press, 1981), p. 58.

I suppose I'm after a kind of grace, or gracefulness. I'm interested in exterior form more than anything else, and while I love wood, I like trees better. I'm not particularly interested in fine details, I want an overall pleasant aspect to my work, an overall richness.[2]

3. Harris, quoted in Pam Bristol, "Two of Ontario's Finest: Karl Schantz and Stephen Harris", *Ontario Craft* (Summer 1987): p. 18.

My work is fairly conservative. I think I'm quite straightforward. I like a clear direction. If a line is curving, I try to find a reason for it, a place to go and a place to return to. I tend to be attracted to things that curve and move, and maybe simulate what I see in natural elements. I probably will always try to use curves rather than geometric shapes. I'm not really comfortable with geometry.[3]

4. Harris, quoted in *The Craftsman's Way*, p. 58.

I think a good piece of furniture is more than good craft—it has something which it shares with good art. You cannot describe the whole thing in one instant because, when you look at it again, there is something else.[4]

Stephen at drawing-board,
c. 1979.

52

Stephen's work could never be called avant-garde. And it certainly wasn't traditional in any sense, other than that the principles underlying it belong in a continuum with what had gone before. His furniture is outspokenly contemporary in feel, makes no questionable compromises with the demands of function, and is warm and friendly to live with. But, perhaps most importantly, much of his work retains a lasting freshness and an inner truth that will not be erased by the passage of time.

Kerry Gordon:

Stephen's furniture has different ways of attracting attention. People who own his furniture will be meeting it and discovering it forever. They will find out things they never knew before, even after ten years. What an incredible pleasure that is. That's what furniture ought to be about. It's just not timeless in the sense of style, it's timeless in the sense that it keeps speaking.

Like the man himself, Stephen's furniture combined seemingly opposite qualities happily joined together in the same frame. Stephen was a quiet, unassuming, almost private man with a gentleness of manner that overlaid the sinews of a surprisingly tough, unswerving will. The furniture he designed is also marked by contrasts; the rigid structure and hard edges are softened by sculptured, curving, organic forms reminiscent of the natural world that was such an important part of his life—the smooth rocks of northern lakes, the twisting branches of trees, rolling fields and flowing water.

. . .

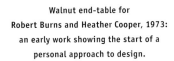

Walnut end-table for
Robert Burns and Heather Cooper, 1973:
an early work showing the start of a
personal approach to design.

The Self-Made Craftsman

In many ways, and in the very best sense, Stephen Harris was a self-made man. Over the years of his youth and early manhood, the values and attitudes he most admired joined a strong will to shape the man who set out in the early Seventies to be a designer and maker of fine furniture. With no formal training and little woodworking experience, other than making props and sets for the stage, he plunged confidently into a craft whose complexities he had yet to face and master. It was a kind of on-the-job training, fraught with an obstacle course of unknowns. He learned from doing, and doing again, until, by sheer determination, he got things not only to work but to work in the way he wanted.

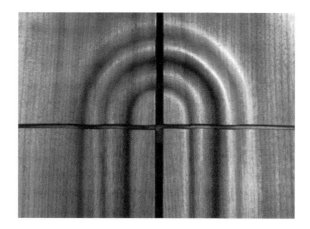

Teaching yourself a craft of any kind is hard, and woodworking, to the highest professional level, is unbelievably difficult in the short time that Stephen allowed himself. From the start, he worked only four years before facing his first serious commissions, usually one piece at a time, never to be repeated, and each one posing its own challenges and problems.

There was much to learn in the early years, not only how to design and build furniture but also about the hardwoods, exotic or otherwise, that he was using, mostly for the first time. Fortunately, Stephen had a knowledgeable friend in Andrew Poynter of Cambridge, Ontario, from whom he bought most of his wood. Andrew had been a woodworker himself, and knew the difficulties, but had become a supplier of special woods to craftsmen all over North America. With an intimate knowledge of woods, he became Stephen's teacher.

From the early 1970s until 1991, the two friends had many lunches together, at which nearly every commission Stephen accepted and the woods to be used were discussed in detail. It was imperative for Stephen to use the right wood

57

**Walnut music cabinet for
Robert Burns and Heather
Cooper, c. 1975.**

for each new job, and to use it properly. All had their own quirky personalities, some more troublesome than others. Is this wood dimensionally stable? Will it behave unpredictably because of inner stresses or uneven moisture content? What might it do when it goes through the planer? Will the internal structure cause surface flaws? After planing, will the wood stay flat? Will the wood's oil content hinder good gluing? Does it take a good finish? Will oxidisation cause a marked colour change? What is the likely waste factor? And so on and so on. It was a new area of expertise for Stephen. The variables in the unfamiliar woods from the remote forests of the world seemed endless. Andrew led Stephen safely through the jungle and the journey became a vital part of his learning. As Andrew knew, Stephen's tendency was to push wood to the limit, and it was as well that he knew what all those limits were.

From his years of working for the English theatre and his own observations, Stephen had acquired a feeling for the highest standards of woodworking. He set himself the same standards and never compromised them, in spite of time-consuming technical obstacles, clients' demands and workshop problems. He knew exactly what he wanted to do, and went directly at it, using his intelligence and the driving will that governed so much in his life. But his standards and his own convictions about how things should be done were applied not only to the job at hand but to his whole working life, to the way he drew, to the design of a piece, to the care and use of tools, the making of the furniture, the whole environment of the workshop. For Stephen, all of it was important, it was all part of living each day the way he wanted to live it.

Once the design for a table or a chair was done Stephen retained in his mind an exact image of how the finished piece should look. That was always paramount. Then the preparatory work began. Stephen particularly enjoyed the preliminaries to the actual making process, the time between the drawing board and the workshop machines, when construction problems had to be

Benge rocking chair originally made as an exhibition piece, 1976. Collection of Patricia and William Harris.

solved. He was a problem-solver, perhaps at times even more drawn to such puzzles than to the often labourious building of the piece. Then, the making of jigs might follow. Stephen could spend two days making a jig for just one cut. The finished jig might often be a beautiful object in itself, but many workshop hours could be used for making it. That was Stephen's way, slow, thoughtful and meticulous in all he did.

He pursued his own route through fine woodworking, sometimes almost regardless of the nature of the material and the recognized good practices of the ancient craft. Wood, the material he worked with, reacts to changes in humidity by movement within its structure. Prudent woodworkers accept this and allow for it in the finished piece. To ignore it is to risk serious consequences, such as cracking. For reasons only he knew, Stephen sometimes did just this and later experienced the all-too-predictable results in the completed furniture.

Perhaps yet more troublesome was Stephen's not infrequent rejection of another woodworking dictum. This says, in effect: use edge-grain for gluing as far as possible, and avoid the end-grain, to which glue adheres poorly. Just as the end of a bunch of drinking straws makes a poor gluing surface, so does the end-grain of wood. Stephen was often told by fellow woodworkers that he relied too much on gluing to end-grain—a practice that will cause a joint to crack most of the time. And, in two cases for early clients, some did. In each case, Stephen had to redo the entire work but, true to his stubborn nature, did them exactly as before. Fortunately for him, everything remained stuck together at the second attempt.

His stubbornness in doing things his way was a hallmark of Stephen's attitude to the material he worked with. He sometimes designed pieces that couldn't or shouldn't have been made because he refused to accept the constraints that others had to deal with. He was often warned about problems but wouldn't

take the advice. He then had to live with the results, even though small compromises might have eased the work without detriment to the final piece. Although Stephen was in many ways a humble man, he was very tenacious and occasionally exposed flashes of strong ego in attitudes to his craft. It was sometimes almost as if he felt that willpower alone could change the physical properties of wood.

Stephen was often plagued by worries, especially when workshop problems were compounded by financial ones. He was highly self-critical, perhaps excessively so, and at times wished he could be more like other successful woodworkers. He particularly admired the achievement of the American craftsman, Wendell Castle, who combined creative ability, good workshop production, efficient business management and remarkably effective self-promotion. Stephen had the first but couldn't achieve the others, and from time to time was upset by this failing in his own workshop.

The problem with money dogged him steadily through his first ten years as a designer/craftsman. In 1976 he wrote in a diary, "It is constantly humiliating to be short of cash. I don't believe I can improve the situation much and make progress in the work at the same time." But he never complained much about money, wasn't jealous of others who had more, and quietly endured the shortage. The nature of his chosen craft and his own approach to it both worked against achieving the kind of income he needed. He charged adequately for the journeyman work he occasionally brought into the workshop to help with cash-flow, but frequently underestimated the time and cost involved in better commissions, resulting in much-reduced profit.

Each commission, by his own choice, was almost always new and demanding, something interesting he had never tackled before. At Sheridan, where some of Stephen's workshop helpers had been trained, they taught a methodical approach to woodworking. Stephen's method was quite different. In his head and on the drawing board he created the form he wanted to make and then struggled to build it so that it held together. When it did, it was like breaking through a barrier. Perhaps he was right not to let technique be too much a dictator. Sometimes, however, he went too far, causing inevitable failures and long delays in completing commissions.

Doug Oliver:

I admire someone like Stephen who had the courage to go his own way. It is easy to stand back and look at it and say it is so impractical, perhaps even stupid. Why don't you set your pride aside a little bit, and learn from other people, get some techniques together, things you can do at a distance? But, you know, Stephen just resolutely went his own way, living his life the way he wanted.

. . .

Three Clients

It was Stephen Harris's good fortune that, in the six years following 1974, three couples came to him with commissions that comprised most of the important work he completed in the first half of his career. Each would discover that Stephen was no ordinary man to whom conventional standards could be applied.

When they first met Stephen, Meri Collier was studying at the Ontario College of Art, and her husband, Dan Perlitz, was deep in his final years at McMaster University Medical School. Neither knew Stephen's work but had heard good reports from friends. They needed a bed and simply asked Stephen to make it. He agreed and showed them a rough sketch.

Cherry chest-of-drawers
originally made as an
exhibition piece, 1974.
Collection of Meri Collier
and Dan Perlitz.

Walnut bookcase with tambour doors for Meri Collier and Dan Perlitz, c. 1975.

English brown oak mirror for Meri Collier and Dan Perlitz, 1978.

M e r i C o l l i e r :

The bed was much lower than normal, but we were students at the time, and gradually moving up from mattresses on the floor, so we accepted the lower bed. It was so different from anything I had pictured. The edges were all rounded, even the drawers underneath. There were no harsh corners anywhere.

Following the bed came commissions for a large dining table and chairs, a book-case, a television cabinet, a mirror, a dining-room cabinet, another dining table and chairs. The first dining table became a conference table in Dan Perlitz's office, and was joined there by a desk, a credenza and filing cabinets. A tall chest-of-drawers by Stephen was also bought directly from an exhibition. The commissions went smoothly but Meri Collier remembers one small difference of opinion.

M e r i   C o l l i e r :

I didn't like the first drawing for the smaller dining-room table. I
insisted that he could change it, but at one point he came back and
said, "I don't think I can design a table for you." It was the only bit
of tension we had. Perhaps I was being too picky, but I think he felt
that he wasn't able to do what I wanted. I have a strong will, and
insisted that he could design a table that would make me happy, and
that he go and do it and he did. I pushed him a little on that, but it
was only a slight thing and we dealt with it very quickly.

**Large cherry dining table for Meri
Collier and Dan Perlitz, 1975.**

66

Collier and Perlitz dining
table extended.

I think it was the softness of Stephen's furniture that appealed to me, and how he moved wood in ways that wood shouldn't move, but part of it was Stephen himself. He was such a beautiful, gentle person. I always enjoyed being around him. Sometimes, after dealing with the work, we would sit around and talk. And I went to his workshop quite a few times; he was just a really wonderful person and his work was part of him, he came as a parcel.

68

Assembly of cherry dining chair for Meri Collier and Dan Perlitz, 1975.

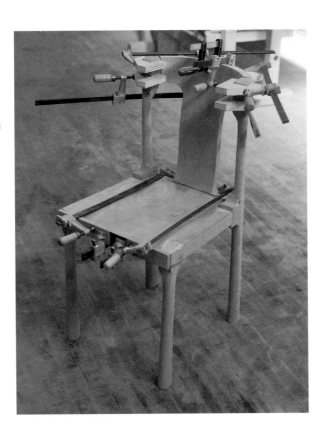

Cherry dining chair for
Meri Collier and Dan
Perlitz, 1975.

Small cherry dining table and chairs for
Meri Collier and Dan Perlitz, 1978.

Detail, small cherry dining table.

Walnut filing cabinets for
Dan Perlitz, c. 1978.

Walnut desk for Dan Perlitz,
1978.

Corner detail of
Perlitz desk.

Dining room in Gorman house.

above:
Gorman dining table, extended.

left:
**Imbuya dining table for Judith and
Richard Gorman, 1979.**

Judith Gorman and her husband, Richard, on a visit to the Perlitz house, had
seen and admired a cherry dining table by Stephen.

J u d i t h   G o r m a n :

I had never seen anything like it. It was almost as if the wood was
folded and there was softness everywhere. Stephen's furniture was
innovative yet timeless. It was both modern and traditional.

The dining table and chairs were the first pieces to be made. Stephen
brought drawings to show us. I had some difficulty understanding
them at first, but Stephen drew very well and, looking back, I think
his beautiful drawings reflected the finished work well.

Imbuya dining chair with upholstered seat for Judith and Richard Gorman, 1980.

76

On the matter of wood, Judith Gorman was much attached to the cherry used in the Perlitz table. So, she said, "Well Stephen, what about cherry?" He replied, "What about imbuya?" She had never heard of imbuya so, she said, "What about walnut?' and Stephen repeated, "What about imbuya?" Then she tried oak and he replied again, "What about imbuya?" Judith Gorman claims to be a slow learner, but it didn't take her long to realize he was going to use imbuya. Once she tuned into the fact he had made up his mind she didn't question his wishes, and grew very fond of the chocolate-brown wood.

Judith Gorman:

Stephen took about a year to make the dining table and six chairs,
so we went quite often to his workshop, sometimes with the children
because we felt it was important for kids today who see eggs in a
carton to know that there is a chicken somewhere and that a person
makes the furniture. We wanted them to see it evolving, and it was
also because of Stephen's personality, the way he worked with wood.
To see him doing it was a very special thing, and we wanted the kids
to see it.

There was something of the Sixties in Stephen's personality but, more
important, he was a bit like his furniture. He was both soft and strong
within. He had a sureness about him. He knew what he was doing. You
knew that you were in good hands. I remember feeling we had hired
an artist, and what's the point if you don't give him some leeway? And
there was a meditative quality, a serenity about him that was real.

Imbuya sideboard for Judith and
Richard Gorman, 1980.

right:
**Walnut and ebony dictionary
stand for Judith and Richard
Gorman, 1981.**

above:
Dictionary stand detail.

The Gormans were embarrassed at the low price they paid for the table and chairs, and when they asked Stephen to make two more chairs he told them he couldn't afford to charge them the same as for the first six. He mentioned a much higher price, and the Gormans agreed because they realized the earlier ones had almost been gifts. It was always a dilemma for Stephen. He felt rightly that he often could not charge what his furniture was worth, but there was equally a limit to how much people would pay.

Heather Cooper and Robert Burns were unlike most of Stephen's other clients, as they both worked in the field of visual design. Quite probably the visual sensitivity of good graphic designers would have increased their understanding of what Stephen was trying to do, and perhaps they contri-buted more than others in the design process. Robert Burns was a great help to Stephen in the early Seventies, being in a sense his first patron, providing both moral and financial support, and urging Stephen, without much success, to promote himself more. Stephen's early pieces at least were photographed, but he was shy about showing them to anyone. Several of his first commissions for both office and house came from these two clients.

Heather Cooper and Stephen certainly seem to have been kindred spirits. They enjoyed each other's company, and found no great problem agreeing on the design of furniture.

**Imbuya stool with wool fabric seat
for Heather Cooper, 1977.**

H e a t h e r   C o o p e r :

Stephen was very understanding from day one when we had little money, right through to the later pieces when we could indulge in some sheer creativity, like the mirror and the stool. Then we said to Stephen, "Go to it." Stephen and I got together and thought, "Now this is strictly free-form, the stool can be anything we like." Neither Stephen nor I, however, was sure it was a very successful piece, thinking it looked too much like a cross between an elephant's foot and a toilet seat.

Because we both worked with our hands, our relationship was less of a client/craftsman thing than one based on what I was doing with my hands and Stephen saying, "Look what I do with mine." We had a common interest.

I often visited his workshop, frequently at his suggestion that I come and look at something he thought would interest me. During the design period, I sometimes took some scribbles with me. He would show me his own sketch proposals, and I would say which one I preferred. Usually he'd say, "I like that one too." That was the extent of it.

Stephen had a vision of what he wanted to do. For a chunk of time, I knew he was hell-bent, and determined that he was going to live his life that way and, by golly, he was not going to compromise. He was a folksy person and a bit of a philosopher who was also an artist, with

East Indian laurel mirror for
Heather Cooper, 1976.

that vision which I am sure he would never have grown out of. There
was a great gentleness in Stephen. He thought hard about things and
he had catholic tastes. Your conversation could just amble around
anywhere. He was such a kind person, and for all the time I knew him
I saw him upset by something perhaps only once.

He used to come over to the house a lot, but after his marriage he was
busy doing other things and drifted away. He was not such a free
spirit any more. I did not see him much in the last few years, but miss
the fact that he is not there. He was an old standby. If I needed something or wanted something made I could always pick up the phone and
say, "Hey Stephen, I've got an idea." It's as if both the individual and
the talent have been nipped in the bud.

· · ·

Walnut television cabinet
for Meri Collier and Dan
Perlitz, 1978.

Working With Stephen

For much of the time in the workshop at 86 Nelson Street, and later in the one on Booth Avenue, Stephen had at least one woodworker helping him. His assistants varied considerably in age, experience, skill and personality but all, if they were to survive, had to adapt themselves as best they could to the workshop environment, the high standards prevailing there and to Stephen himself.

Kerry Gordon:

It wasn't easy to work for Stephen because he designed technically very difficult stuff, and was completely uncompromising. He needed people who were well educated, self-motivated, had the required skill and could make decisions. Some, willing to work as Stephen's helpers, would fall short in one area or another, but he applied the same standards to them as he applied to himself. If he wanted something finished a certain way, he didn't want it sort of like that, he wanted it exactly like that. He was tough.

Cabinet drawer-pulls.

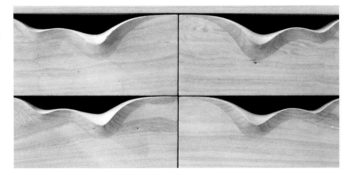

Detail of Collier and Perlitz cabinet door-pulls.

Cherry dining room cabinet
for Meri Collier and Dan
Perlitz, 1981.

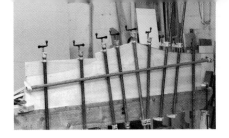

A cabinet side-piece
held by clamps during
gluing.

D o n   C o u l o m b e :

It took me time to get a feeling for his approach to form. He didn't

do technical working drawings. He had such a firm picture in his mind

of what he was doing, he needed the minimum amount of physical

information to execute it. A lot of Stephen's work involved organic

form-transition as one element went into another. You had to get the

feel of that and his sense of proportion—it was almost an intuitive

thing. It took a while. In the first piece I made for Stephen, I did all

the straightforward joinery but could not do the critical junction,

86

Tempered Masonite jig
used for cutting the cabinet
side-pieces precisely to
the required profile.

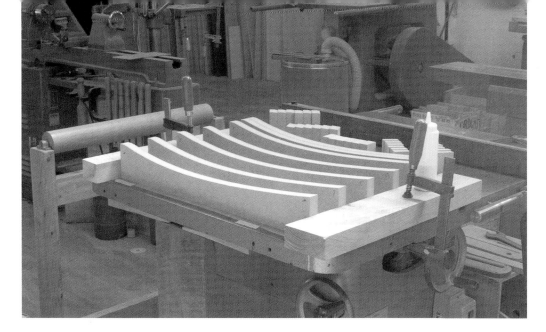

Jig for making curved
cabinet doors.

and made some mistakes. The trouble was that, although I could
design the joint, I had difficulty knowing how much wood to leave for
what had to follow with the spokeshave, rasps, files and sanding so
that the joint arrived finally at the exact finished dimension. It is
really sculpture of a sort and, for Stephen, it was absolutely critical.
It couldn't be a millimetre smaller than he wanted it to be. In the
first chair I made, he judged the legs too spindly. That chair was never
finished, and remained hanging high on the wall of the workshop
until after Stephen's death. I really learned on that piece, and afterwards I made all the chairs in the commission. It just came to me
through doing, how to take Stephen's drawing and turn it into reality.

Walnut stool for
Paul Bennett,
1977.

Imbuya jewellery box, 1982.
Donated by Stephen to auction
for African famine relief.
Collection of Vincent Tovell.

Doug Oliver:

Stephen had very decided ways of doing things, and worked them out
all on his own. He would just come to it out of the blue. He produced
extraordinary work, very well-crafted, but he solved technical problems
his own way, and they didn't always work. He had lots of maquettes for
things that never got off the ground. So he was a little difficult to work
for in that way. It wasn't easy when he handed you a drawing and said,
"Just go and make this."

Cherry dining table for Ruth and John Clayson, 1977.

F r a n k   B o w e n :

Stephen's method of teaching was basically done by dropping you
into a situation to see how you did. He knew it was difficult, and he
wanted to see if you could handle it. I think it is a fair way because
it is really the only way. You gain confidence by achieving, and that is
how he learned himself. He would give you enough room to experience the problems, and make some mistakes. We never argued about
things, but there were occasionally times of trouble when he wasn't
talking to me. A lot of that was simply stress. Training someone to
do work of Stephen's calibre is not easy, and it must have been frus-
trating for him. There was always a point, however, when he would
break off from what he was doing and come to you. You knew he was
upset with you, but he was the one to quell the fire. Stephen was a
humanitarian.

Details of Clayson
dining table.

Clayson dining table,
extended.

Brown settee detail.

Upholstered benge
settee for Alastair
Brown, 1979.

Don Coulombe:

Stephen would often be in debt to the bank to support himself for the
next few months, and then there might be some costly errors or a piece
to be re-made, and that is just devastating when you are on a small cash
flow. He would get severely depressed sometimes. He wouldn't take it
out on anyone, but it might be hard to be around him and although you
wanted to relieve his depression you knew you were helpless to do so.

He had such an impractical approach to his work, even more than
my own. Stephen had no security, and he would still do impractical
things. At that point in my life, I was still engaged in a spiritual
search, and he was really interested in different things that I was
going through. For an entire afternoon, we would sit and talk in the

sun at the second-floor loading doors. I would keep saying: "Stephen,

listen, we have to..., there is this to do and the other...." But he

wouldn't do it; we just stayed there talking, talking about his dreams

and different things. I was amazed that he would think of paying

somebody to talk like that, but for him it was perfectly valid and real.

There was no separation between his work and his life.

STEPHEN HARRIS *Work*

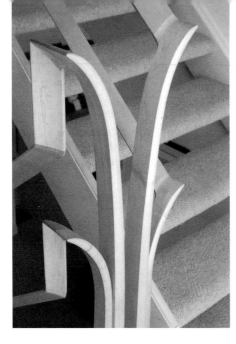

Steam-bent and shaped maple stair railing for Tucker house, Woodbridge, Ontario, 1981.

Once, Stephen was forced to take on a simple job of joinery to bring money into the workshop. Don Coulombe was in the process of carrying out the task, with the same painstaking care he applied to making furniture. Stephen became upset because the work was straightforward and should be turned out faster. Things were going badly and he was under pressure.

Don Coulombe:

He got angry and yelled something at me. Then he returned to the table-saw, where he was pushing through a very large piece of ply-wood. It jammed and flew off the saw. The edge of it hit him on the hipbone, knocking him to the floor. He had a hard time walking after-wards, but we both saw it as a sort of comic reaction to his getting angry at me, and having an accident immediately afterwards. In fact, he said so, but he was still upset, and had to go home because he was unable to work.

Rob Diemert was one year out of Sheridan when he joined Stephen in the workshop.

Rob Diemert:

With most work I did for Stephen, it was back and forth, give-and-take. I would pick his brain, and he would pick mine. That's what I thought was really good about him. I got a sense of being treated equally. There was no sort of put-down or anything like that. We were more interested in getting the work done the best way.

Walnut wall shelf-unit
and low walnut table for
D.K. Tucker, 1982.

97

Once I had a problem I couldn't sort out, and asked him about it. He just looked at me and said, "Well, that's why I hired you." I went back and puzzled over the problem some more, and then he came over and looked at it with me. We discussed various alternatives and chose the best one, whether it was his or mine. The way Stephen put wood together was a lot different from the way other people did. Some of the things Stephen did were just like Stephen himself—unfathomable. It was a bit like, "You can't get there from here."

While working with Stephen, I saw him do things with power tools that I thought at the time were needlessly risky and yet, in retrospect, I'm not sure that they were. I think he was quite calculating about it, and would warn me about certain operations because he had already done them and knew what to expect. He warned me especially about the router templates because it is dangerous to move the router backwards unless you are prepared and braced for what may happen. But one of

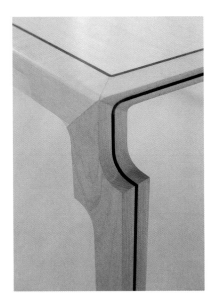

Tucker desk detail.

Maple desk with
imbuya inlay for D.K.
Tucker, 1984.

the things that really stands out in my mind was Stephen talking about working on the table-saw and saying, "You really have to get comfortable with this." I remember doing an operation with the blade up high and unguarded. He reinforced his message several times about being careful, being comfortable with the saw and not being afraid of it. "If you are afraid of it, then something may happen. Maybe the cut's not going to go right or you will have an accident."

Maple hexagonal table with imbuya inlay for D.K. Tucker, c. 1983.

Tucker hexagonal table
detail.

After graduating from Sheridan in 1981, Doug Oliver joined the workshop at 86 Nelson Street to work on his own commissions and speculative pieces arising from a Canada Council grant. During his third year in the workshop he joined Tom Barrett in helping Stephen with a large commission. Michael Fortune was also sharing the workshop at this time, engaged on his own independent commissions.

Doug Oliver:

Stephen's personality was inextricably bound up with the way he worked. They were completely tied together because I think his way of coming to woodworking was such an organic part of him being who he was. For Michael Fortune, by comparison, woodworking is a profession, it is a business. There are ways of approaching business and there are ways of approaching technical problems and so on. You can have strategies to deal with them outside yourself, but Stephen, in a million years, could not do this. With Stephen, it was all internalized,

Tucker table detail.

and came from a kind of knot inside him, particularly design, which was a very slow and painful process for him. Stephen was not a relaxed person, and that made for a certain tension when you were working with him, even sharing the same space. He could get snappish occasionally, although I can't remember any dramatic scenes. He was impatient with people making mistakes, and I made mistakes. His anger, however, passed quickly. He would blow up, snap at you, then half an hour later he would be whistling away. He would be fine and you would still be wondering, "Jesus! I don't know if I want to work here."

STEPHEN HARRIS *Work*

Curly and bird's-eye
maple table for D.K.
Tucker, 1983.

Oak mirror and towel-rail and maple toothbrush holder made by Stephen for his own use, c. 1977.

104

Technically, I'm not sure how much I learned from Stephen, although he talked a lot about woodworking and the right way of doing certain things. For example, I always tended to leave myself a margin for error when cutting wood. I liked to leave some extra material. In cutting a shoulder for something I'd rather make the cut twice. Stephen said, "Have confidence in your hands and yourself. Do it right the first time. Don't fart around."

Stephen's furniture often involved tricky junctions where a complication of multiple surfaces had to fit together all at once and then be carved away to complete the finished corner. To make this possible the joints have to be true all the way down. That demands really accurate work. It didn't seem to scare Stephen but it did me.

Tim Rose worked with Stephen for just one summer in the mid-Eighties before starting at Sheridan. He had little woodworking experience and was only eighteen at the time.

Tim Rose:

Stephen taught me more about life than about woodworking. Woodworking is the kind of thing you learn by doing, as he did. He would let me do as much as I had the enthusiasm and courage for. He eased me gently into more and more difficult parts of a large commission, mostly small pieces on my own that fitted into the larger finished piece being made by others.

I would arrive first, at eight, turn on all the power, the compressor, and get the shop going. We usually finished around six and, although young, I was exhausted at the end of the day. I had a forty-five minute commute in the morning and in the evening, but Stephen could never understand why I wasn't spending my money in bars, carousing and meeting women and whooping it up when the best I could do was get home, make myself some dinner and fall asleep at eight o'clock. He was always bothered by this and used to say, "You're young, you're healthy, you're in the prime of your life, and you should be out enjoying yourself."

Stephen always wanted people who were confident with their abilities and who were prepared to tackle things. It didn't matter too much what their skill-level was. Stephen approached them the same way. He

Cherry conference table,
with wenge inlay, for
the University of Guelph,
Guelph, Ontario, 1984.

still tried to push them further, regardless of their experience. And I know he did this with me. We could not communicate deeply about spiritual or philosophical things because I was so much younger, but we could discuss and solve problems; we were able to focus easily together and find the solution, the best solution. If something wasn't going right, he would stop me, and we would both approach the problem at the same level. It was not Stephen saying, "You are doing this wrong," but more, "How can we do this better?" He treated me as an equal because he was learning too. We were learning every day and, after all, you can learn something from everybody.

Whenever Stephen and I discussed anything, he talked openly and directly without any inhibitions. Even after some difficulty involving Michael Fortune, he didn't really want to talk about it but didn't try to hide it, either. He mentioned it but he wasn't bitter, he wouldn't fight back. He would rather let it go than be aggressive about it. He was never really aggressive, except when he drove. He was never aggressive with people he knew, just with people in other cars.

Shortly after his graduation from Sheridan in 1984, Ian Upjohn was asked to join Stephen at 86 Nelson Street. He was honoured to be asked by Stephen, who, at the end of their interview, said, "I need someone who can do more than sanding and I am confident that you can. So let's just start on Monday."

Ian Upjohn:

I then felt very little confidence in myself as a professional. That was really built under Stephen's support and encouragement. He was one of the nicest employers I've had. He tended to get a little down on himself, as I do also at times. It's very difficult sometimes when you are tired, there is no money, a project is going on and on and there are two depressed people in the workshop. It could be pretty black but Stephen was always very gentle and respectful. He was positive about my work and understanding of mistakes I made. But it was really very difficult to see him beating up on himself psychologically and emotionally.

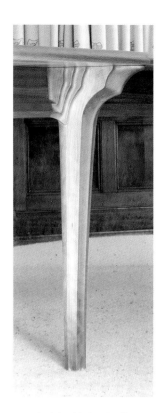

Guelph table-leg detail.

Stephen was very demanding, but I am demanding on myself too, so I think we meshed together very well. He didn't have to encourage me, only to clarify how something should look, and he was very good at that. I learned how to look and how to use my hands, to feel things with the wood, in developing certain levels of sensitivity. I think, more than anything else, that was what I had to learn from him.

Stephen really taught an attitude, and would explain some of the techniques that he had developed to attain certain ends. He would give you a lot of rope, but after a while he might get a bit "antsy" and say, "You really should do it this way, not that other way." But there was a lot of discussion, particularly at the design stage, when he might ask, "How do you think we could do this?" and would listen to what I or others would say.

During Ian Upjohn's time in the workshop, Stephen received a commission from the University of Guelph for a conference table twenty-one feet long. There seemed to be adequate money for the job, but after Stephen designed the table that was no longer the case. And there were some problems, one involving inlay work being done by Ian. He thought it should be done a certain way but wasn't sure and asked Stephen.

Ian Upjohn:

He didn't give me the answer I wanted. I pushed him, and he blew up at me. All he said was, "That's fine," slammed a roll of masking tape down on the table and stalked off to the other side of the shop. I was completely shocked. The question wasn't a big one, and he had never

**Cherry coffee and end tables,
with wenge inlay, for
the University of Guelph,
1984.**

blown up like that before. In thinking about it afterwards, I realized it was a little like a kid asking for his approbation. What I should have done is make the decision myself and it would have been fine. We went out later that afternoon in the car and Stephen apologized. I was amazed that he would do that, because I felt it was really my fault for needling him. But he never pretended it didn't happen. He never let it lie and fester. No matter how painful it had been for him, he would pick it up and resolve it somehow.

Curly maple stepladder with ebony detailing, inlaid rubber treads and spring loaded casters made for Suzanne and David Ivens to use in their showroom, Turn-of-the-Century Lighting, Toronto, 1987.

I think the thing I found most extraordinary about Stephen, and it took me six years to accept, was that he called me his friend. I am very cautious about using that word, and who I dub a friend. With Stephen, it seemed as if friendship was something that didn't end with a few sharp words. It continued. But I didn't feel worthy of that; I didn't feel his equal. Stephen called himself my friend before I felt

Walnut coffee-table made for Daphne Harris, c. 1982.

really comfortable with him. I thought of him really as Stephen Harris, as someone who had less respect for himself at times than I did for him. It took me some time to relinquish that but I did, and he was just waiting for it to happen. It was only much later, when I had a body of my own work behind me, that I felt I had something to offer him in terms of experience, and perhaps technique, that would put our dialogue and our friendship on a more equal basis.

. . .

86 Nelson Street

Of all the woodworkers who spent time in the workshop at 86 Nelson Street, Stephen was the only constant. Helpers came and went, a few others shared the rent, but it was, without any doubt, his workshop. Stephen had found it, assembled the first group who occupied it and imbued it with his personality. He moved there in 1973, about four years after he had begun his career as a woodworker. Many came to share the workshop with him during the next twelve years, until he was forced to move elsewhere. It was an important place for all who worked there, but especially for Stephen, who spent more than half his working life in that bright, spacious, second-floor room. Only six years remained to him when he left it.

Rarely were there finished pieces of furniture in the workshop: once done, they immediately moved out. On the floor sat the work still in progress and an archipelago of purposeful machines, trestles and work-benches. Hardwood was stored vertically against two walls, and festooning the remaining available space were tools, jigs, drawings, rows of clamps, models of joints, and other odd bits that each had once served to solve a problem. Stephen's canoe hung upside-down from the ceiling near the skylight.

Workshop at 86 Nelson Street,
Toronto, c. 1979.

Those who knew the workshop well valued the jigs and models particularly, for they had been made by Stephen with great care, and possessed an intrinsic beauty of their own. Indeed, everything that Stephen did had that personal flavour which made the workshop special. It was a happy place to work, possessing almost a magical quality for some, flowing perhaps from an informal sharing of its space by people doing something they all felt strongly about.

Stephen was clearly the dominant figure in the workshop, having definite ideas about how it should be kept. The others may have had to clean up more often than they liked and keep the space in the order Stephen wanted, but they made the necessary adjustments and hardly ever complained.

Michael Fortune shared the workshop with Stephen for eight years, and next to Stephen was the longest occupant.

Michael Fortune:

I had the highest respect for Stephen's work ethic. He had a well-established routine when he came to the workshop. He sat down for a few minutes with the *Globe and Mail* sports section. Then he would start to work and worked consistently all day. There was no wandering around or indecision about what he was going to do. He was a very steady worker, and as someone just out of Sheridan it influenced me in the way I approached my own work. Stephen had a dedication to the ideas he followed and the process of his craft which was absolutely essential to who and what he was. Though he was often under great pressure, I never saw him compromise. He just accepted the pressure. He could be less than pleasant at those times but he never threw up his hands. He just put his head down and kept on going.

Although they both worked on their own projects, sharing the same space made it apparent over time that the differences between them were marked by more than age and experience. Their attitudes to life and work were not at all in harmony.

Michael Fortune:

Stephen had a very clear sense of what his work space had to be like, even in the sort of music that he wanted to hear. I can appreciate that more now than I did then. I think Stephen and I were good shop-mates for the first six years. But I was ambitious, intent on establishing my career and, in the last two years, I developed my own little professional position, with my own clients. Stephen had a certain way of working, and a certain atmosphere he wanted to maintain in the workshop. You either accepted that or you went somewhere else. Stephen wasn't willing to compromise the nature of his work environment, so it just came apart.

Tom Hurley was a frequent visitor to the workshop at 86 Nelson Street and was sensitive to its unusual quality.

T o m   H u r l e y :

It had a very special feel that I have never found anywhere else. The people there and the space created an atmosphere that was very strong and really quite breathtaking to another craftsman. When Stephen's friends gathered one day to help him move the workshop, it seemed to me a day of some significance, in a sense the end of an era.

For a craft with few communal rites and a scant sense of its own history, that moving day was also a welcome reunion, a chance for the dozen of us to catch up on news and gossip as we tackled the challenges of the day. Those tasks felt familiar to the itinerant wood-workers among us: slinging the jointer under the electric hoist, preventing the dolly from slipping out from under the twenty-inch bandsaw, keeping slivers out of gloveless hands, and packing a pickup like an air-cargo container.

For over a dozen years, Stephen had occupied 86 Nelson Street, al-ways sharing it with two or three other woodworkers. He had shared the shop in other ways, too. As we carried planks down the stairs and sorted the offcuts of bubinga, walnut and cherry, each of us remem-bered special moments. Here was a place you could come for encour-agement, for technical advice, or for help re-sawing a board when

Stephen in the 86 Nelson Street
workshop, c. 1979.

your own bandsaw was down. And here was a shop where the works in progress left you euphoric with a sense of expanded possibilities. That day—moving day—it was still a place where simply running your hands over the jigs, the test joints, and the sinuous bandsaw scraps put you in touch with Stephen's quest for excellence.

Through the Seventies and early Eighties, the inspiration of that room, with its peaked skylights and wood-scented air, had taken many forms. We had crowded one evening onto plank and barrel seats to hear Stephen narrate slides on building his cedar-strip canoe. Over the years, Sheridan College students had regularly toured the shop, clients had come to watch their commissions evolve under Stephen's hand, and journalists had recorded conversations with this shy maker of extraordinary forms.

After the twelve years at 86 Nelson Street, Stephen moved his workshop to a larger space at 35 Booth Avenue. It was in this workshop, over the next six years, that Stephen completed his last commissions. Although lacking the special atmosphere of 86 Nelson Street that was valued so highly by all who knew it, the new workshop had advantages for Stephen; it was not only larger, with good north light, but also had a properly vented spray-room and the luxury of a private washroom. Equally important, it was near where he lived, making lunch at home possible, and not far from the lake where he went happily to boardsail whenever he saw a nearby flag laid out nearly flat by the wind.

· · ·

**Veneer press (6 ft. x 3 ft. bed)
made by Stephen.**

Dessert   Like most craftsmen, Stephen had a strong affection for tools—tools of all kinds, but the simple tools, the direct extensions of the craftsman's hand, held a special fascination for him.

Stephen Harris:

I'll stop at any window that has tools displayed and look at them all, even if they are common things like gardening tools. I suppose anyone who works with his hands tries to get a rhythm going, which is a way of being efficient. If you can get into a rhythm you can just watch yourself work, and certainly good tools, the very best tools, can help you do that. They can be extremely simple but also very beautiful.[1]

1. Harris, quoted in *The Craftsman's Way*, p.58.

Stephen frequently used hand-tools that he had bought or made himself, and housed them in a superb wood cabinet built in the early days of his woodworking career. However, in later years, he more often required the efficiency and speed of air-powered grinders and sanders to carve the forms of his furniture. Yet, at times he faced problems that only another machine could solve. It might be simple or complex but Stephen rarely had the money to buy the commercial equipment designed for such specialized tasks. His way around the problem was often to make them himself.

Stephen was a problem-solver by nature, with an interest in technical things. He therefore embarked on these diversions with pleasure, and often said how much he enjoyed them. Stephen internalized the process of designing furniture and could sometimes be combative about it. The strictly technical problems surrounding a tool, however, did not involve his creative expression or his ego to the same extent, and he could stand outside them in a way that was impossible for him to do with a table or a chair.

Don McKinley of Sheridan College believes that Stephen thought of such interludes as a sort of dessert. I am sure he is right. They relieved him for a time from the personal anxieties of designing furniture, the tension of workshop pressures and the periodic tedium of woodworking itself. They were like little holidays.

The time, sometimes several weeks, spent making a special device was enjoyable, but it was time that wasn't earning money. Yet, unlike many woodworkers, Stephen was self-employed, and had control over his daily existence. He was free, therefore, to indulge himself in work he truly enjoyed, while sacrificing the money that could have been gained in making furniture. It was all part of Stephen living life as he wanted to. Alastair Brown, the filmmaker, felt that Stephen was too good to waste his time this way and chided him during a workshop interview for enjoying too much the excuses for not working. On the tape, Stephen's reply is an irritated grumble and, as one would expect, he continued exactly as he had before.

Apart from the normal shop equipment a woodworker needs, Stephen made a steam-box and boiler which, combined with a clamping table, allowed him to steam-bend wood, a technique opening up entirely new possibilities in the design of his furniture. When he started to work with veneers, he had to make a drum sander to adjust the thickness of veneers to the fine tolerances he couldn't obtain commercially. And, since a veneer-press was also needed for large work, Stephen made one with a bed measuring six feet-by-three, six-inch thick concrete slabs top and bottom, steel chains, cables, and eight fire-hoses lined up side-by-side down its length. It was a crude giant of a thing, far removed from the finesse of woodworking. It was also cumbersome and,

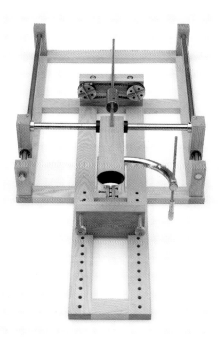

Unsuccessful duplicating jig
made by Stephen.

121

weighing well over a ton, ponderous. Although looking strong enough to withstand any force, the air pressure contained by the hoses was critical. Engineering calculations were checked once again, and the maximum allowable pressure reduced in the interest of safety. In spite of Stephen's concern that this wouldn't be enough, the press, in all its ungainliness, finally performed as it should.

Probably the most noteworthy event among Stephen's technical forays was a duplicating jig on which he laboured during his final commission for the Wandich penthouse. The chairs he had designed for the dining table were, as usual, quite different from anything he had done before, and difficult to make. The eighteen arms, particularly, posed an unusual problem. Their compound curves were to receive a narrow, inlaid band of a lighter-coloured wood. There is no easy way to do this. Stephen could not possibly afford a commercial machine designed for such a job, nor would he seriously have contemplated the alternative of contracting the work out to another shop. His solution was to make the jig himself.

The duplicating jig that Stephen designed and made in oak and stainless steel was an elegant object in itself, but it took seemingly endless time to design and construct. When the moment of truth finally arrived, the jig was found to be hiding a fatal flaw. In spite of all the time spent, Stephen's beautiful jig didn't work. The rotor's cutting head wouldn't track accurately because of excessive bounce in the jig's light structure. This couldn't be fixed easily, and Stephen sadly hung his abandoned labour of love high on the workshop wall, where it remained an intriguing conversation piece until the workshop was finally disbanded. Having failed to create a workable tool for the job, Stephen simply eliminated the problem by making the chair-arms without their intended inlay.

.   .   .

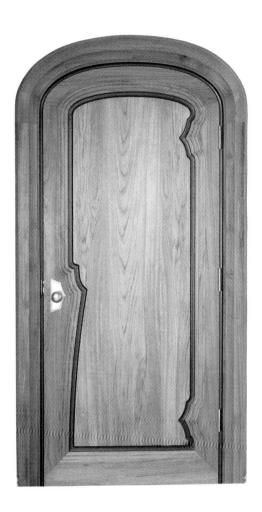

Teak front door, with wenge
inlay, to penthouse for
Alexander Wandich, 1985.

123

The Wandich Penthouse

Nearly all the furniture Stephen made
during his years as a designer/craftsman was for use by clients where they
lived or worked. It was only infrequently exhibited. The most important exhibition in his career was held in 1983 at the Government of Ontario's John
Black Aird Gallery in Toronto, where Stephen's furniture was also shown
with work by Paul Epp, Michael Fortune and Don McKinley. Probably no-
where before had the public and his fellow woodworkers been able to appreciate the full extent of Stephen's abilities.

Cherry-framed mirror doors to
cupboards in Wandich master
bedroom, 1985.

Detail of pull on Wandich
mirror door.

Cherry bed and side-tables
in master bedroom of penthouse
for Alexander Wandich, 1986.

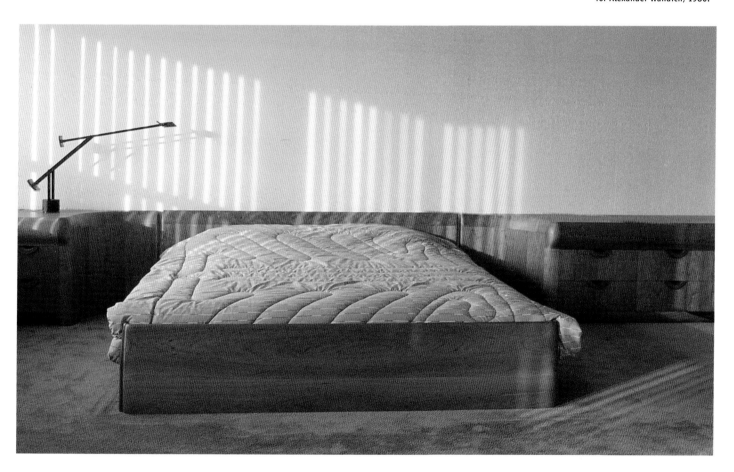

At the time of this exhibition, James Strasman was designing alterations to a penthouse belonging to Alexander Wandich. As the architect, he naturally felt that the renovated penthouse should have well-designed furniture, and his client clearly shared the same thought, for he had already been considering furniture-makers, including the American craftsman Wendell Castle. Jim Strasman, knowing Stephen to be a craftsman of talent, showed Al Wandich slides of his work, and suggested they visit the Aird Gallery exhibition. Al Wandich had never seen Stephen's furniture before, but immediately realized he knew of nothing to match its quality. Shortly after, he talked to Stephen. What followed was the largest and most important commission of Stephen's career. It lasted from 1984 to 1991, when the final pieces were finished. They were the last he was to make.

Cherry cabinets in master
bedroom, c. 1987.

Wandich master bedroom
cabinet detail.

Alexander Wandich came out of a White Russian peasant background. His father had arrived in Canada during the Depression to become a home-steader out west. But times there were bad, so he got on the freights going east, found a job in Toronto and saved enough money to bring three-year-old Alexander and the rest of the family to Canada in 1932. When he grew up, Al Wandich worked as a machinist in Toronto, then moved into real estate and later became the successful developer he is today.

Alexander Wandich is certainly not formed in the normal mould. Jim Strasman has been his architect on several projects and knows him to be an intelligent, serious man with a keen sense of design and an acute awareness of detail. He has acquired an unusual appreciation of architecture and design, gained through travel, his collection of books on the subject, a keen observation and, undoubtedly, through his friendship with Jim Strasman. When the success of the final product in a commission is best assured by both a good client and a good designer, Alexander Wandich could amply fulfil his role as the former. It was certainly so in his association with Stephen Harris.

The master bedroom was the first part of the long commission and the client wanted it to be very special. In discussing the commission, Stephen remarked that he would like to do an entire room. Al Wandich was intrigued by the idea and, as it turned out, Stephen did do the whole master bedroom: the com-modious bed, bedside tables, built-in cupboards under the windows, and a long wall of full-height cupboards behind wood-framed mirrored doors. It is a wonderful room, all the elements coming together to create a spacious, warm and harmonious whole.

Bubinga and wenge guest
bed, with side-tables,
in Wandich penthouse,
c. 1987.

A l   W a n d i c h :

After working with Stephen for some time, I found he had a great
flair in tackling a problem. He really thought about it, he analysed
it. He was sensitive to his surroundings and, although Stephen was
attached to his own designs, he was also anxious to meet my wishes.
He listened. Good designers are often ahead of you and you have
to try and catch up. It is like dealing with a good architect. He will
usually come up with things you will never think of. It should be far
better in the end than you expected.

I was first attracted to Stephen's furniture by the roundness and shape
to it, the fine workmanship. And it wasn't trendy as a lot of work is
these days. You wonder how certain work is going to look ten years
from now and I didn't get that feeling from his. A piece of furniture
must stand the test of time. You should be able to live with it and
always say, "Boy, that's good," and never get tired of it or dislike it.

**Detail, guest bed side-
table, Wandich penthouse,
c. 1987.**

During the seven years he spent working on the Wandich penthouse, Stephen made the front door, the master-bedroom bed and built-in cupboards, beds and cupboards for two other bedrooms, a cabinet, the dining-room table and eight chairs.

Al Wandich:

Once the functional requirements were laid down, I wanted him to present me with his ideas. I didn't want to instil ideas in him. I looked on him as an artist, a creator, and I respected him. If I raised a point about something that bothered me, he might agree but not just for the sake of pleasing me. If he really felt strongly about something he would carefully explain the reason why.

I enjoyed the whole process. It was a lot of fun. I liked being involved in the design stage, to the small extent that I was. Stephen's drawings were so good that whatever he drew was what you got. And I enjoyed going to his workshop to watch him build the pieces and seeing the finished product. Yeah, it was a lot of fun.

When you see what Stephen goes through to produce the final piece, you really appreciate what you're getting. It seemed a challenge to him, as if every piece that he ever did was very, very difficult. He made so many jigs and things, I would think, when I came into the workshop, "Holy Cow! he hasn't even started yet." It was like weeks of building these things, just to prepare himself for starting. It was far from simple. There was always bending or twisting going on, and then perhaps he'd find the wood wasn't right for some reason. He seemed to have no system of production.

Dining room in penthouse of Alexander Wandich.

130

left and above:
Wandich cabinet details.

Mahogany cabinet with pomelle-mahogany top surface for Alexander Wandich, 1988.

Replica of Frank Lloyd
Wright chair.

Early design sketches by
Stephen for Wandich
dining room chair.

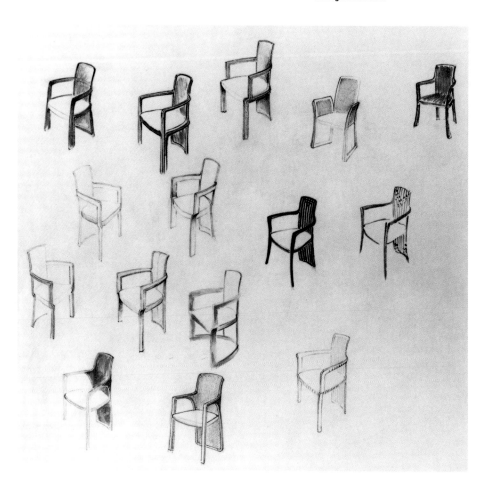

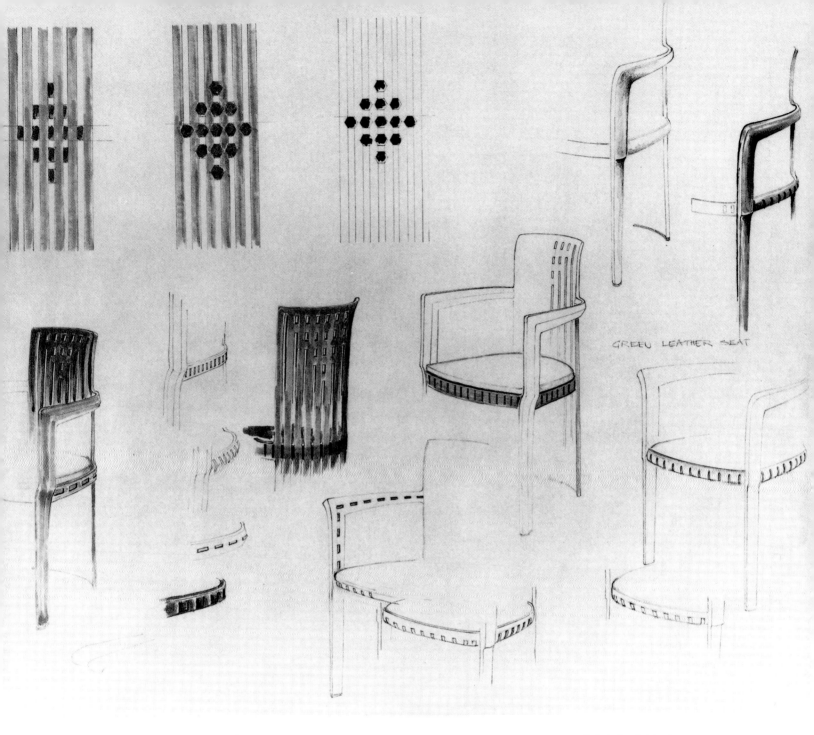

GREEN LEATHER SEAT

**Early design sketches by
Stephen for Wandich
dining room chair.**

Imbuya dining room chair for Alexander Wandich, 1989-90.

Imbuya dining table,
with avodire inlay, for
Alexander Wandich.

Detail of inlaid
edge decoration.

Imbuya dining table,
with avodire inlay, for
Alexander Wandich.

Imbuya dining table,
with avodire inlay, for
Alexander Wandich.

It took Stephen a long time to produce a finished piece. He used to give me an estimate of how long the work would take, but he never met the time, and it was often two to three times his estimate. The work was very tricky and demanding, so it wasn't easy to find good people to help him.

When it came to price, he would think it over, and come up with a quotation. Sometimes it seemed high and I wondered how I was going to live with it, but I knew his work, and said, "Fine, go ahead." I never tried to bargain with Stephen. I wouldn't do that. He was very honest, and, if anything, may have been concerned how high the price was.

Sometimes the quoted price was far too low and Stephen knew he had to ask for more. Not all clients are amenable to such requests or fully aware of the quality in the furniture they are acquiring. Al Wandich was.

. . .

Patterns

Stephen working at a jointer, c. 1979. He was using a jointer when he lost the tip of his finger in a workshop accident.

At the Edge

Ever since the small boy jumped down the laundry chute in his parents' house to find himself imprisoned by the locked door at the bottom, Stephen had a taste for adventure. His sister Marjory remembers him always being the first one up the diving tower, and during the motorbike phase at Upper Canada College, his friends considered him the reckless one. He explored the edge, that jagged outer extreme of good sense where the thrills were to be found, in skiing, skating, diving, flying, riding motorbikes, driving cars, canoeing, boardsailing, or whatever. There is a common thread linking them all, for each in its way is a liberation from static earth, and each involves a world of motion, at times wild motion, in which equilibrium must be won against the powers of wind, water, gravity and other random forces— the kind of personal contest that appealed to Stephen.

Stephen had several accidents on motorbikes, falling off them more than his friends because, as one of them says, "He didn't take note of things." On the Mexican trip, he had a bad tumble. At the time, he was unaware of his close shave with the paralysis often caused by the resulting fracture of a neck vertebra. Only years later was this discovered in an X-ray, taken to assess damage caused by another accident, in which both Stephen and his wife, Daphne, fell over the stair railing in their own house.

On the same Mexican trip, another incident, never fully explained, cast a different light on Stephen and the edge. On a four-lane interstate highway Ian Griffin had stopped beside the road to wait for his friend. Looking back, he saw Stephen approaching rapidly against the traffic in the wrong lanes, swerving wildly to avoid the oncoming cars. It was a highly dangerous game of multiple "chicken" which Ian couldn't explain. It is hard to know what drove Stephen to do this, but it seems more than likely that his nature and youthful daring had propelled him to feel out the rare thrills to be found in such a life-risking experience.

Four wheels didn't appear to be much of an improvement over two. One of his sisters thought Stephen a "terrible car driver," and others talk of scary rides with him. Stephen wrote off two cars, and had a bad accident in a third.

Paul Epp:

To be reckless was important to him and I never quite understood

that. He did have a lot of accidents, and his recklessness was such

that people would refuse to drive with him. I was one of them.

Stephen didn't have the fear that you need to make yourself careful.

He was missing that, somehow. I always felt that he refused to accept the ordinary limits that humans have and it's hard not to see his final accident within the context of many other accidents. For me, it is a troubling thing to think about.

Canoeing and boardsailing caused no accidents but they too, particularly canoeing, were also a test at the limit of prudence. Tom Hurley once returned from a portage to find Stephen about to run some tricky rapids alone. Tom tried to dissuade him because of the danger but didn't succeed. Stephen ran the rapids, remarking later that he just wanted to extend his experience to the limit.

Both in his craft and in his life, Stephen was often drawn to situations, created largely by himself, that put him on the outer edge. In the design and fabrication of furniture he favoured wood because of its warmth and figure,[1] but the organic forms he liked to use were often at odds with its inherently rigid nature. In consequence, he often drove the material beyond reasonable limits and took risks that others would try to avoid. As the problems increased, so did his frustration and his stubbornness to bull things through at all costs.

1. "Figure" is a word used to describe any distinctive appearance in a wood-surface caused by its anatomical structure or irregular colouration.

147

Andrew Poynter:

Stephen pushed things to the edge so far it was as if he almost wanted them to fail. Then he would try and pick up the pieces. There was almost a death-wish in his work. He would do things that should be impossible to do, and yet he did them. But he was risking his reputation or his abilities as a woodworker, both of which were important to him.

Stephen usually managed to conquer these troublesome knots in his work and the equally troublesome knots in himself. With a few exceptions, he managed to put the pieces together in his own way without having them explode later from destructive internal stresses. There were, however, penalties in such risk-taking. Stephen was often tense with the worry and frustration of the difficulties he met in his work. He was a careful worker and experienced with machines but, nevertheless, had more than the normal number of workshop accidents. There were three major ones, all to his hands, one slicing off the top joint of a finger. The last, a deep cut in his thumb from a saw blade, was different from the others. Stephen, for whatever reason, may have precipitated it himself. One Sunday in the late Eighties, he was alone in the shop, working with a table-saw. He later described how he had switched the saw off, turned away from it, then turned back as the blade was slowing down, and stuck his thumb in the saw. Several days later Stephen told me that it was as if he wanted to put his hand in the blade. It didn't sound at all like an accident.

Don Coulombe:

Accidents generally happen when you are scattered, but Stephen, even with his strong will and ego, could push things only so far because of the physical properties of things. He was frustrated by not being able to design pieces that flowed with those physical properties rather than fighting them. It bothered Stephen that the elegance, simplicity and organic form of the final piece were a result of this awkward struggle. It really worried him. He would get a lot of internal tension, and I could almost see him challenge the damn blade, sticking his finger in it, and defying it to cut him.

A longtime friend thought that, as Stephen grew older, he became more physically contemptuous of his own safety. But testing himself to the limit was important to Stephen in a deeper sense. Kerry Gordon understood this "magnetic draw to the edge" because he felt it himself. At the edge, death is not far away, but life is there too. When you are on the edge you are not only testing yourself, you are alive, you are feeling, you are being. Stephen's fascination with the edge and a frequent indifference to risk remained his companions throughout life.

. . .

Water, Rocks, Trees and Wind

Although Stephen often yearned to break free, the working week held him prisoner in the city. But he found an interest in boardsailing (windsurfing), which offered him not only challenge and excitement but the advantage of being within easy reach from workshop or home. At the end of a working day, when the right conditions beckoned, he would race happily and precariously across the Lake Ontario chop. In boisterous winds, this could be a tricky, even hazardous business, but that would be a strong attraction for Stephen. Its principal enjoyment for him, however, was being out in the wind and water of the lake and testing his skill with them on his flighty craft. It was some measure of his progress in the sport that he could eventually manage to sail a more difficult "sinker," so called because of its lower buoyancy.

Of all the ways to be in touch with nature, however, canoeing was his favourite, even his passion. It brought together, in one marvellous package, spectacular scenery, an outdoor life, adventure as risky as one wanted, an often startling intimacy with the wildlife of the north, and the demand for all-weather competence in handling the elegant and sensitive Canadian canoe. Stephen was a skilful and experienced canoeist, not above taking risks when alone, but normally reliable when others were involved.

Making the canoe, 1974.

Throughout the Seventies and Eighties there was rarely a year when Stephen didn't go on a canoe trip in some part of Ontario, no summer being truly complete for him without one. And over six weeks in the summer of 1974, he built himself a beautiful canvas-covered cedar-strip canoe of the traditional design, detailed and made with the craftsmanship and love he could bring to it.

150

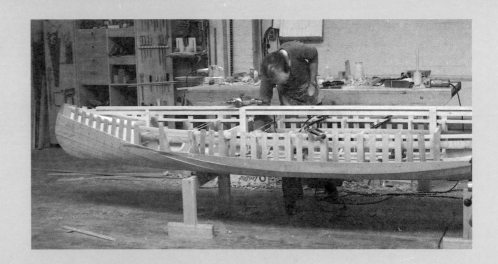

Stephen Harris:

I guess the canoe is the nicest project I've ever done. Perhaps it gains its beauty by default. Something designed to get you from A to B and do it well has got to be honest or it doesn't work; and it has to adhere to natural laws or it doesn't work. I think when one is close to dealing with the world as it is, you then get something good.[1]

1. Harris, quoted in Tom Hurley, "Stephen Harris: Designer/Craftsman", *City and Country Home* (Fall 1988): p. 104

Stephen and the author
launching the canoe
at Canton, 1974.

152

Stephen and his
new canoe.

In 1976 Tom Hurley, a woodworker then sharing the building at 86 Nelson Street, joined Stephen on a twelve-day trip in Nemegosenda Provincial Park, north of Chapleau, Ontario.

Tom Hurley:

I had never gone on a canoe trip like that before and Stephen was very generous in making it happen. He was such a thorough crafts-man in so many ways that he made the backpacks for that trip from scratch, two large, beautifully done canvas packs, complete with everything, including tumplines. The whole trip was quite wonderful and Stephen had such a feel for nature. At one point we were talking about dealing with physical contingencies and I remember him saying that he could probably make what was needed just with the materials nearby. I believed him and it made me feel much more comfortable.

The focus of Stephen's later trips was the north shore of Lake Superior, touted by experts for its superb canoeing. He eventually did six trips on Superior, two alone and the last four with his wife, Daphne. It would be tricky enough canoeing with two paddlers but perhaps foolhardy with only one. The lake is a large, open and unforgiving body of water, notorious for chancy weather and sudden squalls. It's all too easy to imagine the situations one might encounter, with waves rolling in to break against a vertical rock-face offering few places to take shelter.

Daphne.

North shore,
Lake Superior, 1978.

155

Stephen's station-wagon after the accident on the way to a solo canoe trip on the north shore of Lake Superior.

With the canoe tied on top of his car, Stephen was on his way to one solo canoe trip on the north shore of the lake when a car appeared unexpectedly from a side-road. He rammed it broadside, resulting in dreadful damage to both vehicles. His own station-wagon was a complete write-off but Stephen and his canoe were strangely unharmed and able to continue their journey. Stephen's expeditions to Lake Superior always seemed to spawn "incidents" of one kind or another, frightening or dangerous. He said once that, on an early trip alone, he had been wind-bound for several days in a small cove and had experienced a prolonged sensation of extreme fear. It had no obvious cause or rational explanation but affected him profoundly and seemed to be the kind of experience that would linger always in his memory.

Stephen and Daphne did four trips along the north shore of Superior, the first on their honeymoon in 1979 and the last, ten years later, an ambitious plan to paddle out to Michipicoten, an island about six miles off-shore. It was hardly prudent and certainly against conventional canoeing wisdom to attempt a trip of that distance in a fifteen-foot canoe on a lake with such unpredictable weather.

Daphne and Stephen at campsite.

They didn't make it to the island. Wind and rough water drove them ashore against rocks at the foot of a cliff. The waves bounced the heavily loaded canoe around so much they had to stand in the water to hold it away from the rocks. Only later did they find a narrow beach further along the shore, where they managed to spend a miserable night. They were badly shaken by their predicament and all thought of an open-water paddle was abandoned. Stephen knew he had been reckless to involve Daphne in such a venture.

Stephen didn't go back to Lake Superior again, and later told Al Wandich that he had seen a surveyor, orange survey markers and helicopters on his last trip. These signs of what he thought must be imminent mining activity completely threw him off. Stephen wanted to be out in the wild as it had been, untouched by man for thousands of years. Other human beings and their machines spoiled it for him.

. . .

Daphne

Daphne Sherrard and Stephen Harris first met at a Hallowe'en party in the fall of 1978. Glancing across the room, she noticed a face with a particularly warm and welcoming smile. She says it was the smile that got her. And his friends knew exactly what she meant. Stephen's face wasn't a classically handsome one; in fact, it was really quite a strange face, but when it broke into a smile it radiated unusual warmth. Daphne and Stephen soon found they were what each had been looking for. Five weeks after their first date, she accepted his proposal and they were married on 17 August 1979 at St Andrew's-by-the-Lake, on Ward's Island, a ferry ride from downtown Toronto.

Daphne is from Ireland and bears strong hints of that origin in her dark hair and in a complexion so fresh she looks as though she has just returned from a brisk country walk. She grew up in Dublin, where her father was a professor of horticulture at what was then University College, and where her mother was a successful business woman. Her childhood summers were spent by the sea in the south-west of Ireland at Bantry, which became for her what Canton was for Stephen. In the Fifties her parents built a cottage there and it was from this base that Stephen, on several visits, came to know Daphne's many aunts, uncles and cousins and to discover the unique nature of Ireland itself.

157

The paddle made by Stephen
as a wedding present for
Daphne.

Daphne at house of Stephen's
parents, Canton, 1979.

After school in Dublin, followed by four years of boarding school in southern England, Daphne spent several months in Italy and Spain. After this she worked for a year as a nurse and then for two years was employed as a surgeon's secretary, but each summer she returned to Spain to explore the country in the company of Spanish friends. Later, in Canada, Daphne pursued her interest in Spanish language and literature at the University of Toronto, receiving her Bachelor of Arts degree in 1982 and her Master of Arts in Spanish literature a few years later.

Daphne on the day of her graduation from the University of Toronto, 1982.

Daphne emigrated to Canada in 1963 and after two years went to work for the architect Ron Thom, who was then based in Toronto. Over the next few years, she was introduced to two aspects of life that she would later find to be vital parts of Stephen's being. The first was the creative world of the designer searching for excellence in his work, sometimes at considerable personal sacrifice. The second was northern Ontario, its lakes and rivers. Over many years, Daphne and friends explored by canoe the French River and Algonquin and Killarney provincial parks. With Stephen, she would continue canoe voyaging after their marriage. Stephen's wedding present to Daphne was a beautiful cherry paddle he had made for her. It matched one he had made for himself but had small, round decorative elements of inlaid dark-brown imbuya where blade and shaft meet. It symbolized for Daphne the union of two worlds that meant so much to them both.

When she married Stephen, Daphne had been working for some years as a financial consultant to several architects in Toronto, and she continues today in this demanding and responsible work. She was consequently able to bring to the marriage not only love and companionship but also the capital to help them buy a house together. They complemented each other in many ways but, in their life together, Daphne introduced a practical element that Stephen badly needed, as well as a degree of security hitherto unknown to him.

Daphne and Stephen at their
wedding on Ward's Island,
Toronto, 17 August 1979.

159

Even now, when professional career-women are a fact of everyday life, the
old notion of the male as breadwinner still dies hard. It is not always easy
for a man to accept that his stake in the family finances is smaller than his
wife's. Even before the marriage itself, Stephen fretted about this and about
the responsibilities of being married. Afterwards, he continued to worry
about it, although he knew that the situation didn't bother Daphne at all.
Quite to the contrary, she had such admiration and respect for Stephen that
she welcomed the chance to help him in any way she could. For her, this
became an important aspect of their marriage and their friendship.

It was a good marriage, successful for them both, and at times exhilarating,
as Stephen could bring that quality to it. And it was a marriage that had a
marked effect on Stephen. All who knew him noticed the difference. Even his
father, whose relations with Stephen had never been smooth, remarked on

the change in his younger son. After the marriage, Stephen was indeed a new person; he was happier, more relaxed and more comfortable with himself. As a friend has said, "the sun came out." For Stephen, the most important thing was discovering a compatible mate, the successful conclusion of a long search, and the end of a sometimes lonely existence. It was also finding that Daphne could introduce order and a certain degree of security into his day-to-day life. Both greatly eased the worries that had so often in the past ruffled the smooth flow of his work. But more important for Stephen was the fact that Daphne rounded out his life by making it happier and more complete than it had been before.

. . .

The Last Few Months

In the final phase of the Wandich commission, Stephen was to make a dining table and chairs. The client's first thought for the chairs had been a replica of a Frank Lloyd Wright barrel chair available commercially. It was a strong piece, muscular, even chunky in design, but unhappily proportioned. It also looked uncomfortable and, as Al Wandich rightly thought, too architectural. Stephen didn't like to start a commission with the client so strongly influenced in this way and did his own design. Although vaguely recalling the barrel shape of the Wright chair, Stephen's solution was quite different in concept and scale. With light legs and arms curving to meet a richly slatted back extended to the floor, the chair had grace, a quality quite lacking in the Wright replica.

One of the nine Wandich chairs, which took nearly two years to make.

Stephen made nine chairs altogether, one prototype and eight for his client. It is a fine chair but its construction was complex, involving many pieces of imbuya, almost every one cut to its special size, shaped to its own jig, and steam-bent. Each chair required an immense amount of work before it was ready for assembly, gluing, and final finishing. Only then could the upholstered seat be installed.

Stephen's workshop spent the better part of two years on the chairs alone, and the dining table still remained. Kerry Gordon, an experienced woodworker with years behind him working with, among others, the internationally recognized craftsman, Krenov, was in the workshop when the chairs were made.

Kerry Gordon:

The chairs were incredible pieces of design. They look simple but, having watched Stephen build them, I know that they were the most technically difficult objects I have ever seen. The amount of discipline involved was extraordinary. Stephen was completely uncompromising. With all those jigs and all the work, that chair was never going to happen again. It was done, complete, finished—one-of-a-kind.

With all woodworking, indeed in most crafts, there is a tedious phase when it is sometimes hard to keep going. Stephen had become familiar with this, but in the last year or so he seemed to be going through something more fundamental—a loss of enthusiasm and drive. He became fed up with the pressure of work, perhaps brought on, as Kerry Gordon suggests, by the huge task of making the difficult Wandich chairs. To other woodworkers, who sensed that he was losing interest, Stephen talked about the work becoming tiresome. Kerry Gordon saw the change that came over him when he could escape and put the workshop away for a while to go boardsailing. Stephen appeared ten years younger as he looked forward to the pleasure of testing himself against the wind and the waves of the lake.

As the last commission came to an end, with no others yet in sight, he talked about the future in one of his darker moments. He wondered if the workshop might have to close down and, if it did, whether he would have the energy to start all over again. The pressure of the long Wandich commission could easily have spawned this state of mind, and it might not have lasted long but Stephen still faced real though not insurmountable problems. His tenure of the workshop had become uncertain because of renovations being carried out by the building's new owners. Another move, with all its disruption and expense, was therefore a possibility in the not too distant future. Kerry Gordon, who had shared the workshop for several years, was leaving not only the shop but woodworking as well, and Stephen would have to find someone to replace him. In spite of these factors, the lack of new clients and his own possibly transient low spirits, Stephen was still able to talk optimistically to Daphne of overcoming the problems, staying in the workshop as long as he could, and obtaining enough grants to do his own work for an exhibition he hoped to have within two years.

Whatever the outcome might have been, he and Daphne had planned for some time to renovate their house. For the summer months of 1991, at least, he could take a break from the workshop and its problems to concentrate on the immediate, practical business of making their house more livable. On occasion, he had told me how much he would like to renovate a house. During those last months Stephen had his chance. Sadly, he never saw the work finished.

. . .

His Own Man

For a few years before going to England in 1963, Stephen Harris was seriously engaged in ordering the values he would carry with him in life. But finding the right way through the ethical thicket posed by the world he faced wasn't at all easy for a young man. He was lucky, therefore, to have as a friend someone who became a strong influence during this important time. Terry Casey must have been an unusual man. Four years older than Stephen but more mature than in age alone, he was well-educated, well-read, and already an architect. In addition, Terry had explored in depth the nature of integrity, a problem with which Stephen was then grappling. In a real sense, they were both on the same path. Terry recognized this, became interested in Stephen and acted during those years as his friend and mentor.

Holding strong views about integrity, Terry applied them widely—to people, literature, art, music, and much else, even machines. As the two became friends, he noticed that Stephen sometimes erred in making such judgements about his own actions or those of others. Feeling Stephen was at times in danger of fooling himself, Terry tried to show him where he had gone wrong. Stephen didn't like the intellectual discipline Terry imposed, but it was good teaching from a man Stephen respected, and it sharpened Stephen's awareness of what integrity really meant. It was to be a valuable asset in Stephen's career as a craftsman.

When Stephen returned to Toronto in 1969 he was thirty, close to a decision about the years ahead, and had shaped the person who would live them. From boyhood battles with a strict father, from his free-wheeling youth, and from the young maverick's stand-off with authority and the formative five years in England, Stephen the man finally emerged, coded in part by heredity but, with Terry Casey's help, tailored more than a little to his own pattern.

The deep rebellious veins that troubled his family had been transmuted, over time, into adult strengths. And Stephen had acquired, as he grew up and matured, an attitude of mind and a personality that was to permeate his work, his relations with others, and the way he lived. Stephen was, in fact, a man quite out of the ordinary: an original, with qualities that were to be savoured, enjoyed and respected by all who knew him. He had become an indivisible whole, determined to live and work in a way wholly consistent with his beliefs. This was not a matter of style, something contrived for a purpose. It was far deeper. It was the very essence of Stephen, and simply flowed out of him.

But there also were puzzling contradictions in his make-up that sometimes flashed to the surface like dark glints in its matrix. Stephen's natural gentleness of manner could be shattered at times by impetuous outbursts, even

short flashes of temper. His innate consideration for others sometimes abandoned him entirely behind the wheel of his car, and he was not the kind of
man who could tolerate those who didn't command his respect. At work, he
was hard on himself almost to the point of masochism, a complex personal
involution that often added unnecessary stress to his life. And the strong will
that did so much for him in other ways could sometimes descend into an
unreasoning obduracy that became a hindrance rather than a help. Yet another
of those dark glints was the strange seduction that drew him towards extreme
challenge in work and life.

Although Stephen achieved much as a craftsman, it was Stephen the man who
probably had the greater impact on others during his short life. All those he
touched as friends, clients or fellow woodworkers had respect for him. Most
experienced at first hand his honesty, his outstanding integrity, his tenacity,
the warmth of his friendship, his generous nature and his sensitivity to the
feelings of fellow beings.

Stephen was very discriminating about almost everything in his life and this was especially true with friends. He didn't make close friends easily. They had to prove themselves on his own terms first before they were accepted. It was not an easy process, because Stephen was a complex person, and sometimes difficult to read. The friendships arrived slowly and were probably the better for that.

Apart from woodworkers, Stephen had friends and broad interests in fields unrelated to his work. He could talk about art, music, football, food or anything else of one's choosing. He was a good companion, in canoe or in workshop, with a light-footed sense of humour and, at times, a boyish enjoyment of play, brought out by Bill Hayes in the dog days of one summer when he and Stephen played fiercely competitive games of make-shift paddle ball in the cluttered workshop.

Stephen was often in debt during his first ten years as a craftsman, but even in hard times he didn't complain and his concern for others always remained a vital part of the man he was. His whole life was sprinkled with kindnesses and acts of thoughtful generosity. He played the role of elder brother to young craftsmen, lent tools to others, gave warm clothes to a needy man on a cold winter day and once reduced his scarce financial reserves to help another with a gift of his fare home to Calgary. Stephen's concern for others was genuine and often practical, but it could also be expressed on an entirely different level.

Ted Hodgetts:

It is a great gift to be generous with your enthusiasm. That is something that is good to remember about Stephen. I will never forget his encouragement of what I did and still try to do. It meant a great deal to me at a certain point in my life, especially coming from him.

In daily life, Stephen carried himself with ease and self-assurance, meeting others more often than not, with his engaging smile. All who knew him remember that smile; it radiated the gentle nature of the man. It is not surprising that words like "gentleman," "old-fashioned" and "courtliness" are used by his friends in talking about him. In his manners and the way he treated others, all of these could apply, but not just in their superficial meaning. With Stephen, relations with others were only the outward and visible expression of the person he was, right through. What one saw was what Stephen was. There was never any pretense.

In light of his talent and growing reputation, Stephen remained throughout his career a humble man, with an ego held in check and largely focused on his craft. He was fully aware of what he was and was capable of doing, but he was modest about his accomplishments and never pushed himself or tried very hard for the recognition he deserved.

What was true of Stephen the craftsman was equally true of Stephen the man. They were indivisible. The same attention to detail, the same sensitivity and the same restraint were applied to everything he did, even the little things of life like the simple clothes he wore.

Don Coulombe:

I liked how Stephen searched for truth not only in his work but in other areas of his life. That is why he lived so simply. He wanted things basic and real and he treated people wonderfully. His attitude to other humans and his sense of values were in every way consistent in his life.

. . .

Twenty-two Years

Twenty-two years is not a long working life. At thirty, Stephen Harris started late, and, at fifty-two, he died young. In that short span, his achievement was remarkable. To advance so rapidly, in four or five years, from someone merely competent with woodworking tools to a designer/craftsman of high quality, is quite outstanding.

What made it possible were Stephen's attitude of mind, his relentless determination, and the late-blooming talent he brought to his craft. With their help, he made phenomenal progress in his skills, his ability to draw, and the evolution of his own particular style of furniture. He did this working mainly alone, at a time when few others in Canada were designing and building contemporary furniture to Stephen's high standards.

His path on this journey was quite different from that of most other woodworkers. Sheridan College's Don McKinley describes Stephen's approach to his work, using a track-and-field analogy. He compares the many woodworkers engaged in the "flash and dazzle" of javelin or discus with Stephen, deeply and totally absorbed in a long-distance run, the long run of his personal quest. Stephen did not meander through life discovering things more or less by accident. He was in search of his own goals with a sharply focused dedication, rejecting out of hand anything that deflected him from that lonely course. This was his route through the twenty-two years of his career, a long, probing pursuit of the truths to be found in his craft, in the furniture he made, in himself.

This personal search and single-minded resolve fortified him and infused his work with its special quality. It was a lonely experience at times and, for Stephen, not truly shared by anyone, even the helpers in his workshop. He alone was responsible for the concept of each piece, for bringing it to fruition in the right way, for the time it took to make and for its cost both to him and his client.

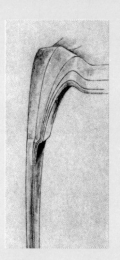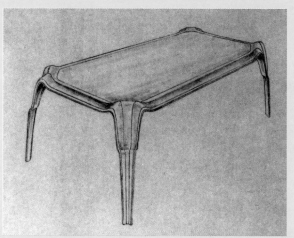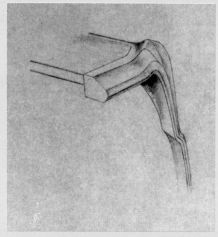

In the early years, Stephen was virtually a pioneer, one of very few in the country practising his craft in the way he did, and with little support, apart from his few clients. He persevered doggedly on his solo marathon, producing over time a small but distinguished body of work. He liked it that way, often selecting solutions quite different, in some respects, from anything he had done before. Thus, each piece tended to stand on its own, complete in itself, but behind them all lay a careful, quiet craftsmanship that was unexcelled and absolutely uncompromising.

169

Although Stephen often took liberties with wood that others might not, he clearly liked the material, exploiting the warmth and tactile qualities of the beautiful materials he used. He was loyal to the demands of function and, with few exceptions, rarely distorted basic form beyond reasonable limits; he relied mainly on the shape of members and their carefully considered line to establish the personality of each piece. Corner joints, where vertical and horizontal meet, were important to him and often received carved embellishment for emphasis. Few hard edges or corners occur; the rounding of them and the use of curves tame and soften the rigid, linear quality of the wood. In general, Stephen's work is conservative, owing something to tradition mainly in its restraint. Aggressive modernity is absent, as is any hint of the superficial or the trendy that mars so much of contemporary work.

Increasingly, as Stephen gained confidence, the various elements of a piece were lightened. Only the required amount of wood was used, and more thought was given to the subtleties of line in the delineation of form, on transitions and junctions. He also began to focus on surface-decoration, experimenting with patterns created by incising and inlaying. The final results were graceful pieces, strong in form, relieved with curves and a subdued enrichment of detail. Shining through it all was an impeccable craftsmanship. Stephen's furniture was in a class of its own, unequalled at the time in Canada, and able to stand with the best anywhere.

By the time Stephen hit his stride in the 1970s, he had acquired a reputation among the group of friends, clients and woodworkers who knew about him. That was soon to spread through exhibitions and magazine articles. The Canada Council had already recognized his importance in 1976 with an arts grant for travel and study in Europe, the first ever given to a woodworker. He exhibited work and received various awards during the Seventies and Eighties. His work was also honoured by acquisition for the permanent collections of the Chalmers Foundation, the Massey Foundation, and the Ontario Crafts Council, the first two of which are in the Canadian Museum of Civilization, Hull, Quebec.

In a society that pays little attention to its fine craftsmen, Stephen may have received his reasonable share of recognition, but it is certain that he could have gained more through self-promotion. He was, however, not that kind of man and shied away from pushing himself. It was only in the later years, when he was beginning to feel that his true worth wasn't being acknowledged, that he tried to organize an important exhibition with the woodturner Ted Hodgetts and the instrument-maker Linda Manzer. In the end, he found the negotiations not only time-consuming but irksome, and abandoned the whole idea, feeling resentful that the quality of the work alone didn't justify an exhibition without the hassles of promoting it. Stephen and others of his quality certainly deserve wider acclaim, but attitudes in Canada are not yet attuned to the value of such craftsmen.

Stephen Hogbin:

For me, the Seventies had two important figures in the development of furniture: Stephen Harris as the studio designer/craftsman and Don McKinley as the instructor of a generation of furniture designers and makers. This continued until the beginning of the Nineties.

**Stephen, the author and "Joss"
at Durham House, Canton.**

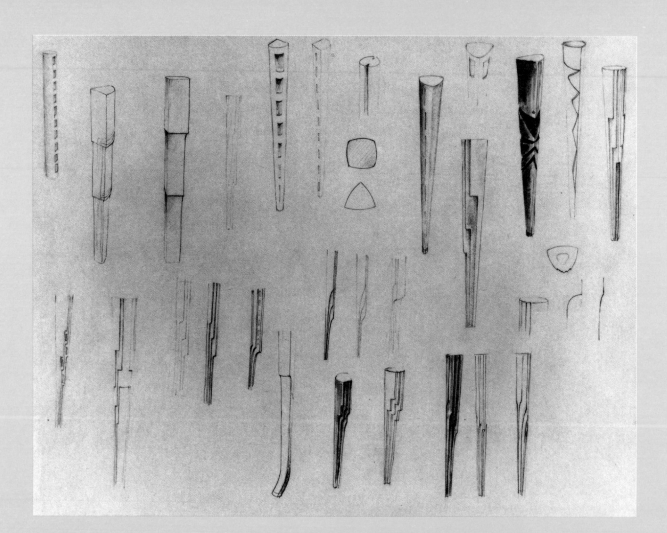

Studies by Stephen for the design
of a table-leg.

Paul Epp:

Stephen has a unique and special place. He was the senior art furniture-maker of the modern era in Canada. He was a pioneer here and
didn't have many peers. His work was as good as anyone's anywhere.

In spite of its singing quality, the body of Stephen's furniture is not widely known. He made relatively few pieces, one at a time, and most are now in private hands. Stephen's career came to an end when he was at the peak of his profession. His legacy, however, is difficult to assess. Even during his life, Stephen's influence was projected in a narrow beam and affected only a small number of people. The volume of work he produced was too low to have a wider impact and what he did make was seen by relatively few: woodworkers and clients mainly, a few friends, the readers of the occasional magazine article on him, and the viewers of the rare exhibitions in which he showed. His style was so personal that his work doesn't fit easily into any known school, nor is it likely to have many followers. But the mark he made was unique in the world of Canadian woodworking and added a different dimension to it.

Beyond the value of his own work, Stephen Harris was an important model for the young woodworkers coming out of Sheridan. His workshop was a kind of postgraduate course. For many, it provided their first experience of what high standards really mean in practice, and what is necessary to achieve them. They were also able to see at first hand how one man was able to do this in the Toronto of the time, and still manage to make a sort of living. It gave them hope about their own futures, although few, in fact, would be able to duplicate Stephen's precarious balancing act.

Stephen in 1990.

Daphne and Stephen at Durham House, Canton, 1987.

174

Stephen Harris was an unforgettable man endowed with the qualities that fostered lasting friendship and warm affection. His legacy resides in the furniture he made and, most vividly, in the memories of all those he touched during his life. Of these, the designers and makers of furniture form a separate group, for they had a special understanding of Stephen, the man and the craftsman.

Ian Upjohn:

For me, the most important thing is that Stephen was a model for me. He was not only honest with himself but also in tune with himself and his abilities. Something I very much miss now is knowing that there is someone in the world like Stephen who could turn within and connect with something. He wasn't just floundering around. I have never seen the work of any other furniture-maker that has his integrity or exceeds his standards, here or elsewhere.

. . .

Stephen Harris

Born:

Toronto, Ontario, 8 June 1939.

Education:

Forest Hill Public School and Collegiate Institute;
Upper Canada College; Ontario: grade thirteen.

1961-1962: University of New Brunswick, Fredericton: one year, General Arts.

1963-1968: London, England: freelance set-design, property-making; worked in many West End theatres, including the Royal Court Theatre, the National Theatre and the Royal Opera House, Covent Garden.

1968-1969: Property-maker on staff of Drama Department, University of Alberta, Edmonton

1969-1991: Designer/craftsman making wood furniture for private clients.

Died:

Toronto, 20 August 1991

Teaching experience:

1977, 1980-1981: Part-time instructor, furniture studio, School of Crafts and Design, Sheridan College, Oakville, Ontario.

Lectures/slide presentations:

Ontario College of Art, Toronto
School for American Craftsmen, Rochester Institute of
  Technology, Rochester, New York
Holland College, Prince Edward Island
Humber College of Applied Arts and Technology, Toronto
Wendell Castle Workshop, Scotsville, New York

Exhibitions:

Canadian Guild of Crafts:

1971 Canadian National Exhibition, Toronto
1972 *Make*
1973 Interior Design Show
1974 Two-man show, Craft Gallery
1975 *Ontario Master Craftsmen*
1976 *Crossroads*

The Craft Collaborative:

1976 *Excellence in the Making*, First Canadian Place, Toronto

Participant-organized show:

1983 *Recent Works by Four Furniture-Maker*s, John Black Aird
  Gallery, MacDonald Block, Queen's Park, Toronto.

Collections:

The Chalmers Foundation Collection, Canadian Museum of
  Civilization, Hull, Quebec
The Massey Foundation Collection, Canadian Museum of
  Civilization, Hull, Quebec
The Ontario Crafts Council, Toronto

Awards and Grants:

Design Canada Craft Awards:

1974 Award of Merit

Ontario Crafts Council:

1975 Grant for purchase of equipment
1976 Grant for purchase of equipment

Ontario Arts Council:

1983 Arts Grant
1988 Grant for purchase of equipment
1991 Grant for purchase of equipment

The Canada Council:

1976 Arts Grant for travel and research in Europe on Charles
     Rennie Macintosh and Antonio Gaudi.
1983 Project-Cost Grant

The Ontario Association of Architects:

1988 Allied Arts Medal

Publications on Stephen Harris:

"Gallery-Stephen Harris." *Ontario Living* (June 1988).
Garner, Philippe. *Twentieth-Century Furniture*. New York:
     Van Nostrand-Reinhold, 1980. (stool for Heather Cooper)
Hurley, Tom. "Furniture Makers in Toronto." *Fine
     Woodworking* (November-December 1988).
     . "Stephen Harris. Designer/Craftsman." *City and
     Country Home* (Fall 1983): p. 101-4.
Massey, Hart and Flanders, John . *The Craftsman's Way*.
     Toronto: University of Toronto Press, 1981, p. 58.
Strasman, James. "Flowing Forms: Furniture Design by Stephen
     Harris." *The Canadian Architect* (October 1985).

The following were interviewed
during research for this book:

Family

Ruth Clayson
Daphne Harrris
Howard Harris
Marjory Harris

Clients

Alastair Brown
Meri Collier
Heather Cooper
Judith Gorman
Ken Tucker
Alexander Wandich

**Woodworkers
and friends**

Frank Bowen
Geraldine and Peter Carter
Don Coulombe
Charles Coutts
Michael Cruickshank
Rob Diemert
Chris Dobson
Paul Epp
Ian Griffin
William Hayes (by letter)
Ted Hodgetts

Michael Fortune
Kerry Gordon
Stephen Hogbin (by letter)
Tom Hurley
Don McKinley
Doug Oliver
Andrew Poynter
Dominique and Ray Prince
Tim Rose
James Strasman
Ian Upjohn